Models for the Preparation of America's Teachers

by Donald R. Cruickshank

The Phi Delta Kappa Educational Foundation
Bloomington, Indiana

Cover design by Charmaine Dapena

Library of Congress Catalog Card Number 84-62616
ISBN 0-87367-430-8
Copyright © 1985 by the Phi Delta Kappa Educational Foundation
Bloomington, Indiana

Dedication

This book is dedicated to the primary stakeholders in teacher education, including teacher educators, heads of teacher education units, university presidents, members of accrediting and certification units in state departments of education, superintendents of public instruction, members of teacher education accrediting agencies, staff members of teacher education organizations, staff members of unified teacher organizations, members of interested federal agencies, and, of course, America's teachers.

This monograph is sponsored by the University of Southern California Chapter of Phi Delta Kappa, which made a generous contribution toward publication costs.

Table of Contents

Introduction

Teacher education is big business. Each year more than 100,000 aspiring teachers are graduated from over 1,200 colleges and universities in the United States. Many of them join the two million teachers currently in the work force. The education of teachers is not only big business, it is important business to a democratic nation that depends on an educated citizenry.

Who are America's teachers and how are they educated? What is their curriculum? As we proceed through the Eighties, it is an opportune time to look at the teacher education curriculum in American colleges and universities. In this volume I shall survey curriculum and instruction in preservice (undergraduate) teacher education in order to reveal the state of the art, to identify issues and problems, and to submit suggestions for improvement. But before examining curriculum and instruction in preservice education, it might be helpful to consider the components of teacher education by using an analogy with the theater.

First there are the actors on the stage — undergraduates and their mentors, both teacher educators and academicians. Backstage there are staff support persons, largely clerical. Offstage are the producers, directors, and set decorators — namely university presidents, heads of teacher education programs, and other administrators. Out front is the audience — school people, parents, and the general public. The analogy with theater falters somewhat when it comes to the playwright and script, but it could be said that these are the function of those who create and implement the teacher education curriculum.

A truly great play requires, among other things, fine actors, outstanding sets, skillful management, sensitive direction, and an excellent script. When theater awards are distributed, there tends to be one award to play A for best acting, another to play B for set decoration, and so forth. Occasionally a play comes along that wins almost all the honors, but that is the exception. Great plays are great because they assemble all the proper ingredients and utilize them in the proper proportions. Mediocre plays are mediocre because they have some good components and some bad. Plays that fold quickly usually have little or nothing to recommend them.

The above analogy suggests that if teacher education is to become great, it must have all the components of great theater. Unfortunately, this has never been the case for sufficient, if not good, reasons. It is doubtful that teacher education has ever had enough good actors — students and teacher educators — because, among other things, the play "Teacher Education" is a spectacular that requires a large cast but has a very low budget. Nor has it had a stage that is functional and attractive. Furthermore, the scripts written by and for teacher educators are accused of being shallow, and the acting "method" is questioned. Finally, producers and directors of teacher education seem at times to be mere stage managers rather than insightful and sensitive leaders of the craft.

The analogy may also suggest the work that must be accomplished, namely: to improve the selection of the actors (preservice teachers and teacher educators), to improve the script and the acting (preservice curriculum and instruction), to improve the sets (the contexts and facilities for preservice education), to improve the stage crew (support personnel), to improve the selection and preparation of the directors and producers (administrators of teacher education programs), and most importantly, to convince the audience that doing these things will be to its benefit. In this volume, I shall focus on only two of the several components mentioned above: the teacher education curriculum and instruction in teacher education. Obviously, more must be attended to before teacher education can achieve its potential.

Part I, "The Teacher Education Curriculum," presents an overview of the current practice in the preservice curriculum. It considers both the general and professional education requirements of prospective teachers, notes related problems and issues, and raises questions or makes suggestions for resolving them.

Part II, "Alternative Teacher Education Curricula," provides truncated reviews of 22 newer ideas for the preservice curriculum, most of which have received only brief or minimal attention from teacher education practitioners. These alternative proposals were gleaned from the writings of such individuals as James Conant, Arthur Combs, Frances Fuller, Robert Travers, B. O. Smith, Charles Silberman, and Mortimer Adler; from such programs as the TEAM project, Teacher Corps, Comprehensive Elementary Teacher Education Models, Competency-based Teacher Education, Study Commission on Undergraduate Education, Multicultural Teacher Education, The AACTE Bicentennial Commission Report, *Educating a Profession: Profile of a Beginning Teacher*, and the NEA report *Excellence in Our Schools: Teacher Educa-*

tion; and from research on teacher effectiveness.

Part III, "Instruction in Teacher Education," focuses on teaching method and instructional alternatives, with attention to such questions as: What promising instructional alternatives are available for use in preservice teacher education? and What alternative instructional materials are available? The major alternatives highlighted are microteaching, simulation, Reflective Teaching, and use of protocol materials. Included is a description of each with sections on user reactions, related research, advantages and disadvantages, and support materials. Additional instructional alternatives and materials are identified using work done by Wesley Meierhenry, Robert Houston and colleagues, the Stanford Center for Research on Teaching, the National Education Association, Frederick Erickson and Jan Wilson, and Meredith Gall.

Part IV, "Summing Up," synthesizes the many suggestions made throughout the volume and thus might serve as an agenda for improving preservice curriculum and instruction in teacher education.

Donald R. Cruickshank
July 1984

Part I

The Teacher Education Curriculum

Education as an academic discipline has poor credentials. Relying on other fields, especially psychology, for its principal substance, it has not yet developed a corpus of knowledge and technique of sufficient scope and power . . . to be given full academic status.

James D. Koerner
The Miseducation of American Teachers
1963, p. 17

The teacher education curriculum comprises two parts: *general education* and *professional education*. General education is one of several terms used to define the education that is purported to be of value to all persons. Professional education, on the other hand, is used to define the education needed to practice in a particular profession. In education it is referred to as pedagogy or the art and science of teaching.

For as long as formal teacher education has existed, there has been conflict between academicians and teacher educators over the balance of general versus professional content in the undergraduate teacher education curriculum. Academicians believe that general education and knowledge of the discipline to be taught should be the only prerequisites for holding a teaching position. Most teacher educators, on the other hand, maintain that additionally there is a common body of knowledge about teaching and learning that all prospective teachers must acquire.

While the conflict persists, in practice there has been an uneasy truce wherein academicians more or less oversee general education and the academic content for the teacher's teaching specialty, while teacher educators control

4

pedagogy. From time to time, there have been efforts to reach a compromise with proposals to extend the period of teacher preparation from the current four years to five or even six years so that teacher education students could receive both more general and professional education (AACTE 1982; Smith 1980).

General Education

The te:ms general education, general studies, or liberal arts education often are used synonymously although they have different origins and somewhat different meanings. The concept of the liberal arts derives from third century B.C. Greece with subsequent modifications, especially in the sixteenth century. Historically the liberal arts were seen as studies deemed most fitting only for freemen or citizens of Greece. Emphases then were on learning to think and to converse. Such studies expanded from the *trivium* (logic, grammar, and rhetoric) to include the *quadrivium* (arithmetic, geometry, astronomy, and music). Together they came to be called the "seven liberal arts." The essential common denominator of these early studies was that they were not intended directly to prepare persons for vocations. Over time other studies either replaced some of the above or were added. They included psychology, sociology, natural science, and modern foreign languages.

During the nineteenth and early twentieth centuries the liberal arts increasingly fell into disregard as a result of several emerging phenomena that shifted interest from learning for its own sake (knowledge as its own end) to learning in order to perform (knowledge as a means to an end). Among the emerging phenomena were industrialization, the scientific revolution, universal suffrage, and mass education. Individually and collectively such events were key factors that caused increased interest in vocational or specialized education, including professional education for teachers.

In addition, respected intellectuals became critical of classical studies. John Dewey, for example, in *Democracy and Education* (1916) emphasizes that liberal studies had their origins in slave societies and are no longer appropriate. He argues that liberal education in a democracy should give "individuals a personal interest in social relationships and control and the habits of mind which secure social changes without introducing disorder." Thus a liberal education increasingly would be related to the problems and realities of a democratic society.

Because the term "liberal arts" had fallen into disfavor, the Harvard Committee on General Education (1945) introduced the term "general education" to avoid both the classical and elitist connotations associated with liberal arts education. General education was proposed as the means of preparing an individual to be a free person and citizen. It was an education designed to give a person the capacity to examine his or her life, a sense of inner freedom, and a broad outlook in order to overcome provincialism. The curriculum that would

5

contribute to these ends was said to consist of the natural sciences (understanding of the physical environment and human beings' relationship to it), the social sciences (understanding of the social environment and human beings' relationship to it), and the humanities (understanding of human beings themselves in their evolution and ways of thinking).

More recently, Phenix (1964) defines general education as the search for human meaning and understanding that results in a complete person, a humanized person. Phenix suggests that a curriculum in general education falls into six "realms of meaning," namely: symbolics (ordinary language and mathematics), empirics (physical, natural, and biological sciences), esthetics (the arts and literature), synnoetics (personal knowledge), ethics (moral knowledge), and synoptics (history, religion, and philosophy). Persons so educated would be skilled in speech, symbol, and gesture; factually informed; capable of creating and appreciating objects of aesthetic significance; endowed with a rich disciplined life in relationship to self and others; and able to make wise decisions, to judge between right and wrong, and to possess an integrative outlook.

At about the same time, Conant (1963) describes a liberal education both as a process and as an aspiration:

> A liberal education, one might say, is a process begun in childhood, carried on through a varying number of years of schooling, and best tested by the momentum it sustains in adult life. It is characterized by what it aspires to, rather than by what it embraces; it aims to enlarge the understanding, to develop respect for data and to strengthen the ability to think and act rationally. . . . It seeks to produce an informed, inquiring and judicious habit of mind rather than particular abilities. (p. 92)

Adler (1982) suggests that a "liberal and general" course of study needs to permeate grades K-12 and must include acquisition of knowledge in three areas: language, literature, and fine arts; mathematics and natural sciences; and history, geography, and social studies. Why these three? Because, says Adler, "They compress the most fundamental branches of learning. No one can claim to be educated who is not reasonably well acquainted with all three" (p. 24).

Silberman (1970) provides a "test" to determine whether a particular study is liberal.

> What determines whether a particular study is liberal is the way it is taught and even more, the purpose to which it is taught. . . . Is its purpose to enlarge the student's humanity and his understanding of the role and purpose of knowledge? (p. 388)

More recently, in an effort to counteract the drift away from general education, Harvard University in 1978 proposed a redesigned general education program that requires students to select 10 semester-length courses within five precisely defined academic areas: literature and the arts, history, social and

6

philosophical analysis, science and mathematics, and foreign culture (Seligman & Malamud 1978, p. 61).

On most campuses the general education curriculum still follows notions contained in the earlier Harvard Committee Report (1945) and consists of courses in the social sciences, natural sciences, and humanities. But according to Silberman (1970), such courses are all too often taught with a narrowly professional or technical purpose in mind and are designed to train professional historians, mathematicians, physicists, and so forth. In fact, general education requirements for undergraduates on most campuses are not usually very specific. That is, rather than exact course requirements, there are only general stipulations. For example, at Ohio State University, 45 quarter hours of general education credit are required, 15 each in the humanities, natural sciences, and social sciences. Many universities readily admit that they do not offer anything resembling a true general education. Instead they refer to the requirements simply as basic education requirements.

The demise of general education on university campuses has been attributed to many things, including lack of interest on the part of students. Sewall (1982) asks:

> Do the liberal studies — that is, the bodies of knowledge that include language, mathematics, science, history, civics and the fine arts — still possess enough authority to capture the imagination of young people easily diverted by more sensate activities? Could yet another generation largely indifferent to mental exertion and precision inflict irreparable damage on a citizen-propelled polity and an information-based economy? Should we brace ourselves for a plague of cultural amnesia? (p. 603)

Additionally, general education has been hurt by lack of interest on the part of employers and a loss of interest in teaching undergraduates by faculty who operate under a reward system based on research and publications. In recent years Boyer and Levine (1981) and Winter, McClelland, and Stewart (1981) have made a strong case for reviving general education on university campuses.

All in all, general education suffers from a malaise. The cure will require a redefinition and re-evaluation of general education. If general education is to be successful it must be more clearly defined and valued. In the absence of the above requisites, undergraduates will continue to take courses to fulfill basic education requirements that in reality are either beginning courses intended for those going on to pursue a major in that discipline or courses that are intended to be remedial, that is, to make up for lack of general education in high school.

General Education and Teacher Education

There is a common expectation that teachers should have a broad general education because they are collectively responsible for the formal general

7

education of youth. They also are expected to serve as models of well-educated persons for youth and for the community at large. Additionally, if teachers are generally well educated, they can draw on that "reserve" to enrich their own teaching specialty. Such assumptions have led all institutions preparing preservice teachers to require that one-third or more of the curriculum be in general education. Gutek (1970) says of such programs:

> Although the general education requirement is found in all teacher education programs, it varies a great deal in quality. Some institutions have developed well-thought-out programs of general education, while others have programs of poor quality which consist merely of accumulating numbers of credit hours in something vaguely labeled "liberal arts." (p. 140)

Provision for the general education of teachers has the sanction of teacher education accrediting, approval, and certification bodies such as the National Council for Accreditation of Teacher Education (NCATE) and state education departments. Nearly three decades ago, NCATE (Armstrong 1957) began to make its position on general education clear when it stated:

> Ideally . . . all persons in our society should be well-educated. For the teacher, however, being well-educated is a necessity. Without it, the teacher cannot interpret any field of knowledge in its proper relationship to the whole of society, and without it, the teacher will not be respected by a society which is itself becoming increasingly well-educated. . . . The committee believes . . . that being a well-educated person is so essential to the satisfactory performance of the functions of a teacher at all levels as to justify an emphasis on liberal education at the preservice level. (p. 9)

Nevertheless, general education for teachers is still defined and addressed only scantily in the more recent teacher education literature. For example, the NCATE *Standards for the Accreditation of Teacher Education* (1982) define general education simply as the "studies most widely generalizable." According to NCATE, such studies should be taught "with emphasis upon generalization rather than the academic specialization as a primary objective" (p. 15). The "studies most widely generalizable" are proposed to be symbolics (communication through symbols) including studies in languages, communication skills, linguistics, mathematics, logic, and information theory; natural and behavioral sciences; and humanities. NCATE notes further that these studies should constitute a minimum of one-third of the total coursework of future teachers. This breaks down into approximately 40 or 60 credit hours for semester and quarter systems respectively.

General education for teachers also is addressed briefly in the National Association of State Directors of Teacher Education and Certification (NASDTEC) *Standards for State Approval of Teacher Education* (1981). NASDTEC defines general education as follows:

8

General education is that component of a teacher education program providing the knowledge, skills, understandings and appreciations associated with a well-educated, sensitive individual. (p. 17)

Accordingly, the general education curriculum would include:

the study of the liberal arts which embraces the humanities, fine arts, mathematics, natural and behavioral sciences. . . . General education is not defined by subject matter alone but rather by an attitude toward the world which emphasizes intelligent functioning as a human being. (p. 17)

Conant (1963) provides a clearer rationale for the inclusion of general studies in the teacher education program.

There is moreover, an important practical reason for certain studies: almost any teacher inevitably faces the necessity of dealing with subjects outside his area of specialization, not only in his classroom but also in conversation with students. If he is largely ignorant or uninformed, he can do much harm. Moreover, if the teachers in a school system are to be a group of learned persons cooperating together, they should have as much intellectual experience in common as possible, and any teacher who has not studied in a variety of fields in college will always feel far out of his depth when talking with a colleague who is the high school teacher in a field other than his own.

And too, if teachers are to be considered as learned persons in their communities (as they are in certain European countries), and if they are to command the respect of the professional men and women they meet, they must be prepared to discuss difficult topics. This requires a certain level of sophistication. For example, to participate in any but the most superficial conversations about the impact of science on our culture, one must have at some time wrestled with the problems of the theory of knowledge. The same is true when it comes to the discussion of current issues. (pp. 93-94)

Conant goes on to address directly the amount and content of general education for teachers. He suggests that, "assuming a good high school preparation," general education should occupy half of the student's time for four years, and that it should be a "broad *academic* [as opposed to vocational] education." Figure 1 is an illustration of what Conant recommends as general education for teachers.

Silberman (1970) addresses the liberal education of teachers in his controversial book, *Crisis in the Classroom.* He contends that teachers must have a firm sense of direction, a commitment to the preservation and enlargement of human values, and the ability to transmit that commitment to youth. Teachers must be educated to self-scrutiny, self-examination, self-renewal, and to serious thought about purpose. He supports courses for teachers that would show them how knowledge is developed and how humans may differ in their approaches to inquiry. Silberman, like others, believes it is the joint

Subjects already studied in high school	Number of Courses	Equivalent Semester Hours
The English language and composition	2	6
The Western world's literary tradition	2	6
History (at least one-half other than American)	3	9
Art appreciation and music appreciation	2	6
Mathematics	2	6
Science (physical and biological, each studied consecutively)	4	12
Subjects not studied in school		
Introduction to general psychology	1	3
Introduction to sociology and anthropology	1	3
Introduction to the problems of philosophy	1	3
Introduction to economics	1	3
Introduction to political science	1	3
	20	60

Figure 1. Components of a general education program recommended by James Conant. From *The Education of American Teachers* (New York: McGraw-Hill, 1963).

responsibility of colleges of education and academic departments to work toward these ends; but he claims that the academics have refused to take the job seriously.

B. O. Smith, in "The Liberal Arts and Teacher Education" (1971), claims that if liberal arts are again to play an important role in the education of teachers, they must come to grips with modern day experience as persons in a mass society experience it. Such studies must move out of the classroom into the field in order to view individuals confronting the social, political, and economic issues in their experience. They must find ways that ventilate problems and acknowledge the interdisciplinary character of events in daily life. Persons must be subjected to fresh interpretations of their problems, purpose, and social destiny. They must establish a set of norms to use in addressing problems and issues that confront them from day to day.

Howsam, Corrigan, Denemark, and Nash (1976) in the AACTE Bicentennial Commission Report, *Educating a Profession*, state that general education should help teachers become learned persons because they are responsible for the intellectual development of children. Consequently, they "must be interested in ideas and capable of understanding them in broad conceptual contexts" (p. 82). The authors recommend that prospective teachers participate in experiences that focus on the nature and implications of knowledge that are provided by an interdisciplinary team. Therein students,

> will consider alternative ways of knowing, unique structures of knowledge in different fields, linkages among concepts in various

disciplines, and the implications of these ideas for teaching in the elementary and secondary school. (p. 82)

Ten years after he first addressed the topic, B. O. Smith (1980), in outlining the ingredients of a teacher education curriculum, is increasingly suspect and critical of general education.

Schools of pedagogy no less than the nonpedagogical schools and departments have been, and continue to be, possessed by the magic of the expression "general education." The referent even in the most stringent definitions is elusive. Its meanings are as numerous as the points of view regarding what education is all about. To some it means dipping into a number of disciplines, tasting general courses here and there; to others it means pursuing a program in the humanities which strangely enough often skirts philosophy, the integrative discipline par excellence.

As a result of preoccupation with the notion of general education, a considerable proportion of the prospective teacher's academic program, sometimes amounting to half of the credit hours, has been distributed over a large number of fields from which the student has acquired only very superficial knowledge. Because of the term's ambiguity and vagueness and the tendency of those who use "general education" to stand for a little of this and a little of that, the term will not be used [in my book] to designate any part of the professional curriculum for school personnel. (pp. 31-32)

Instead Smith goes on to argue for in-depth preparation of prospective teachers both in the subject matter they will be required to teach and in "complementary areas." Thus, in the latter instance, a prospective secondary teacher of physics would study philosophy of science since it would complement a science teacher's curriculum. He proposes use of a "categorization of knowledge" developed by Tykociner from which the complementary knowledge for any teaching field could be selected. Thus, Smith replaces the concept of general education with the concept of complementary knowledge. Careful selection of coursework from this array of complementary knowledge will enable teaching candidates,

to discuss . . . questions of personal and intellectual significance, to serve as a model for an educated person, and to increase the possibility of continued intellectual growth. (p. 32)

Academicians, as would be expected, support the need to educate teachers generally. Ritsch (1981) proclaims:

I suggest that education has as a necessary function in the preparation of teachers the constant application of the processes of thinking and activities of understanding to the form and substance of the liberal arts disciplines. Certainly a primary aim of teachers is the communication of the availability, place, meanings, and values of those knowledges which are the foci of liberal arts disciplines to those who have had little or no contact with these disciplines as areas of significant human knowledge. Thus, education must, in the training of teachers, demand that prospective teachers come to grips with such basic questions as: "What does this or that particular area of knowledge mean?" "What basic sets of questions and historical context gave rise to this or that particular area of concentrated knowledge, and what is the place of this or that concentrated knowledge today?" "What methods, skills, and value concerns have resulted from the shaping and elaboration of this or that discipline, and how do these relate to other disciplines or areas of knowledge?" All such questions lead toward such fundamental concerns of teacher preparation as "How and when do I, as a teacher, go about preparing students to comprehend and then undertake studies in this or that area of knowledge?" and "What do these disciplines or areas of knowledge have to offer that might improve efforts to teach, contribute to learning, and improve understanding of the social, historical, and philosophical contexts of schooling?" These are, for the most part, questions which are not central to the concerns of the liberal arts professors, yet which are, or should be, vital concerns of the prospective teacher, especially elementary and middle school teachers. (pp. 408-409)

A smaller number of academicians believe that possession of a general education should be the *sole* criterion for entry into teaching. Mortimer Adler is among that number. In the *Paideia Proposal* (1982), he calls for a single-track system of public education that provides all children K-12 with the same curriculum with virtually no electives and no vocational training. That curriculum would consist of fundamental knowledge (history, literature, language, mathematics, science, and fine arts), basic intellectual skills (reading, writing, mathematical computation, and scientific investigation), and the enlargement of understanding (aesthetic appreciation of works of art, ability to think critically). In addition, Adler proposes 12 years of physical education, eight years of varied manual arts (cooking, typing, auto repair), and at least one year focusing on choosing a career. Since the Paideia curriculum contains the "general learning that should be the possession of all human beings," Adler proposes that its teachers must receive a solid liberal arts education and "the hell with courses in pedagogy and educational philosophy" (Stengel 1982).

The public, too, expects teachers to be well-educated persons. Unfortunately, in some instances teachers have been viewed as not even basically educated in the three R's. A much referred to article in the 16 June 1980 issue of *Time* magazine, "Help! Teachers Can't Teach!" is illustrative of how too many of the public view teachers.

Quite a few teachers, estimates range to twenty percent, simply have not mastered the basic skills in reading, writing and arithmetic that they are supposed to teach. (p. 55)

Recently various states have announced their intention to ensure that teachers be well-educated persons, or at least be competent in the basics, by mandating teacher competency tests. For example, Florida requires teacher candidates to pass the Florida Teacher Certification Examination (Department of Education 1982), which contains subtests in reading, writing, mathematics, and professional education. Oklahoma similarly examines teacher candidates, but in their major and minor approval areas. For example, a prospective teacher of algebra is examined both on algebra and on general mathematics. Many other states have similar bills before their legislatures. In addition, many states have mandated that prior to admission to teacher education programs, candidates must demonstrate basic competencies as evidenced by scores on standardized tests such as the Scholastic Aptitude Test (SAT), the American College Testing Program Assessment Test (ACT), or the California Achievement Test (CAT) (Ward 1981).

Adding fuel to the legislative fires, a Boston University professor reported that he found high school seniors who planned to major in education, compared with seniors who planned other majors, well below average both in verbal and math scores on the SAT (Weaver 1979).

In conclusion, the public, teacher educators, and academicians agree that teachers should be well educated. However, general education, and particularly the general education of teachers, has seen hard times and suffers from neglect. Over the years, some persons and institutions have made efforts to revive or resurrect general education. Only a few of these voices have been listened to and fewer yet heeded.

In order to improve the general education of teachers, the following questions need to be addressed. Can general education be redefined or reinterpreted in a way that has common acceptance and that will provide direction? How much general education is necessary relative to the total curriculum for teachers? What should constitute the general education curriculum for teachers? Can what is envisioned be brought into reality? How can education students and faculty alike be drawn toward general education? How can teacher education accrediting and approval agencies be made more interested in the general education of teachers? How well are current preservice teachers being generally educated? Finally, are generally educated teachers more effective teachers by any standard?

Professional Education

The term professional education implies education for a profession. However, whether teaching can be considered a profession has been at issue for decades. Ornstein (1981) enumerates 13 commonly cited characteristics of a profession, four of which are considered to be most important. They are: 1) a defined body of knowledge beyond the grasp of the public, 2) control over licensing (certification) and entry requirements, 3) autonomy in making decisions, and 4) high prestige and economic standing.

Whenever teaching is compared to such lists of professional characteristics, the consistent conclusion is that it lags well behind such professions as medicine and law (Howsam et al. 1976; Schein 1972). Howsam (1980) summarizes:

> the evidence seems to indicate very convincingly that teaching, as it presently exists and functions, manifests the characteristics of a semi-profession. It is clear, however, that in the nature of its contributions and its societal function it *is* a profession. To the extent that it performs below its potential, the schools and society are losers. (p. 94)

If a primary criterion for any profession is that it possess a distinctive body of knowledge, then professional education would be "a specialized body of knowledge and skills . . . acquired during a prolonged period of education and training" (Schein 1972, p. 8). Such studies obviously would differ among professions. In law, that knowledge is contained in courses on appellate practice, contracts, torts, and property. In medicine, professional knowledge and skill are gained in courses in cardiology, endocrinology, and pathophysiology. In education, courses such as tests and measurement, curriculum theory, and diagnosis of learning problems are offered. The essential common denominator of these courses is that generally they are *not* intended to be of interest to persons outside the profession.

This essential body of knowledge necessarily would be agreed on and accepted within the profession. It would be compiled and organized in some form of index or manual for ease of access, similar to the physician's desk reference.

Having a distinctive body of knowledge and knowing better than anyone else how it should be applied, that is, what is good for the client, ensures that only those possessing that knowledge would be capable of decision making in that realm. Following from this, a profession would need to have control over practitioner licensing, control of entry requirements into the profession, autonomy, and prestige.

The most serious obstacle preventing teaching from having true professional status is the lack of consensus among educators regarding what constitutes the requisite specialized body of knowledge and skills for effective teaching. For example, whereas Ohio State University College of Medicine lists more than 20 courses, individual studies, and seminars, the College of Education lists well over 300. Even accepting that the two fields are different and that education may be more inclusive and more diverse, surely medicine has more concurrence regarding a basic professional culture than does education.

Armstrong (1957) elaborates on the lack of consensus among teacher educators regarding a core professional culture.

> The lack of curriculum pattern indicates that the faculty of an institution has given no systematic thought to what should be included in a teacher education program; that the faculty is unwilling to back its own judg-

ment; or that it believes no pattern is necessary. Whatever the reason, it is likely to result in gaps in the academic and professional education taken by students, in undesirable overlapping of content, in having students at different stages of their educational programs enrolled in the same courses, and in intensifying the problems of evaluation. (p. 6)

A second obstacle interfering with education being perceived as a true profession is that a teacher's education is acquired within a four-year undergraduate program, rather than during a prolonged period as with law and medicine. Over the past several decades, proposals have been put forth to extend preservice programs, but they encounter difficulties and soon are shelved. The first difficulty already has been mentioned. The profession simply does not agree on what teachers must know to begin practice, and therefore there is no scope and sequence to curricula that would justify prolonged preparation. A second difficulty is the belief on the part of many, including teacher educators, that prolonged preparation of teachers is not warranted economically. They ask, "Why would young people expend so much time and effort to become a teacher when the economic rewards are so low?" A third difficulty confronting the professional requisite of prolonged preparation is the historical dichotomy between preservice and inservice education. Do some now — do some later.

Before professional education will be taken as seriously by others as teacher educators would desire, those responsible for it must redefine and re-evaluate what exists. If consensus can be achieved regarding what professional knowledge and skill count, then the general public and academicians will grant increasing autonomy and respect to educators.

Professionalizing Education and Teacher Education

All we have to exhibit is a plethora of course titles and programs . . . and practice guided by bandwagons and publicity. (Broudy 1963, p. 45)

Course work in education deserves its ill repute. It is moot, often puerile, repetitious, dull and ambiguous — incontestably. Two factors make it this way: the limitations of the instructor and the limitations of the subject matter that has been remorselessly fragmented, subdivided, and inflated, and that in many cases was not adequate in its uninflated state. (Koerner 1963, p. 18)

Regardless of the professional status of teaching, professional education goes on and has gone on since the early nineteenth century when pedagogy — the study of the art and science of teaching — emerged as a distinct and specialized field of study (Borrowman 1966, p. 1). Prior to that time, study in a liberal arts college was considered the only necessary preparation for teaching, since students would be exposed to the best available knowledge. This was in the tradition of the medieval university that, when bestowing the arts degree, in essence, admitted the holder into the guild of professional teachers. During and after that time, three distinct trends developed that, when understood, help to illuminate the emergence of professional education (Borrowman 1966; Silberman 1970).

One trend occurred on university campuses in the nineteenth century where the liberal arts curriculum was undergoing expansion, diversification, and even occupational specialization. By the end of the century, some university scholars agreed that the study of human development, the learning process, and educational institutions were legitimate undertakings within the framework of liberal studies. The arguments included: that the study of education could be scholarly if it yielded valuable insights for rational human behavior, that education as taught in the university was a liberal art or science, and that technical or craft training then being offered to younger students in the emerging normal schools was fundamentally different from the liberal-professional education that could be offered potential educational leaders in a university (Borrowman 1966, pp. 11-13). President Eliot of Harvard made a case for admitting new disciplines into higher education and subsequently established a chair of pedagogy.

A second trend occurred with the development of normal schools, which provided from two weeks to two years of a highly technical curriculum intended to beget immediate, practical results, that is, to funnel trained teachers into America's fast-growing common school classrooms.

> The latter half of the nineteenth century saw the appearance of a crusade to professionalize teaching, led by Horace Mann, Calvin Stowe, James G. Carter and Edmund Dwight. . . . So bitter was the resistance of liberal arts colleges, yet so strong was the determination of the American people to provide better training for teachers that state legislatures established, as they were forced to do in the field of agriculture, separate institutions to provide professional preparation for teaching. Consequently the normal school which later became the teachers college [and still later the multipurpose state university college] was created. (Chandler, Powell, and Hazzard 1971, p. 158)

The general intention of the normal school curriculum was to focus solely on and contribute to successful teaching performance.

A third trend was the conciliation of the differences between those who championed liberal education and those who advocated only professional education. Persons in this conciliatory school of thought believed that future teachers should be exposed to both liberal and professional education, and that both could be brought together within the baccalaureate degree. Without question the conciliators won out, and professional education — that which is considered unique to the preparation of teachers — has been placed, likely permanently, in juxtaposition with general studies, mostly within the four-year university curriculum.

Today most persons, including academicians, agree that teachers need to be professionally educated, for they alone are responsible for knowing formally how to educate others. Whitehead proclaims, "We are only just realizing that the art and science of education require a study and genius of their own; and that this genius and this science are more than a bare knowledge of some branch of science or literature" (1949, p. 16). Silberman notes, "The question is not whether teachers should receive special preparation for teaching, but what kind of preparation they should receive" (1970, p. 413).

All institutions preparing preservice teachers now require that some coursework be taken in professional education. The disagreement occurs mostly over the nature and amount of the preservice education curriculum. Conant (1963), in his study of 77 institutions in 22 states, notes a few constants in teacher education curricula: educational psychology, at least one methods course, one course related to the function of the school in society, and student teaching. Relatedly, he reports that semester-hour professional course requirements for elementary majors range from 26 to 59 and for secondary majors from 17 to 30 (p. 125).

Chandler et al. (1971) estimate that about 15% of the work required for legal certification of high school teachers is devoted to the study of pedagogy and the practice of teaching under supervision. Similarly, they estimate the median for state certification for elementary teachers at 20% (p. 160). More recently, Sherwin (1974), in her study of 719 institutions, finds the professional curriculum to be divided between psychological and social foundations and curriculum and instruction. Within the psychological and social foundations area, educational psychology is required most often. Sherwin reports that elementary majors have course requirements ranging from 26 to 35 semester hours, and secondary majors have course requirements ranging from 16 to 25 hours (p. 15). As would be expected, special professional education for teachers is mandated by teacher education accrediting, approval, and certification bodies. For example, the NCATE *Standards* (1982) note:

> The professional part of a curriculum designed to prepare teachers should be distinguishable from the general studies component. The general studies component includes whatever instruction is desirable for all students regardless of their prospective occupations; the professional component covers all the attitudes, knowledge, and skills required of a teacher. (p. 16)

According to NCATE, those abilities requisite to becoming a teacher can be (but need not necessarily be) subsumed under four categories of professional studies. They are: 1) content for the teaching specialty, 2) humanistic and behavioral studies, 3) teaching and learning theory, and 4) practicum. Across the entire preservice curriculum, multicultural education and special education requirements have recently been mandated. Since almost all notable teacher education units seek NCATE accreditation, their programs meet or follow the standards. Thus, in a sense, the NCATE curriculum can be likened to a modal curriculum for preservice education.

Content for the Teaching Specialty

> Only through pursuing a subject well beyond the introductory level can a [prospective teacher] gain a coherent picture of the subject . . . so that . . . he can communicate something of the spirit to others. (Conant 1963, p. 106)

The "content for the teaching specialty" is also referred to as the teacher's subject area, concentration, or teaching major. For elementary and secondary preservice teachers, the content for teaching specialty is comprised essentially of the subjects to be taught in the schools. Prospective elementary teachers would study the elementary school curriculum. The National Association of State Directors of Teacher Education and Certification (NASDTEC) *Standards* (1981) for elementary teachers note:

> The program shall require study designed to develop knowledge in the subject areas normally found in the elementary school curriculum including art, health, mathematics, music, physical education, science and social studies. (p. 37)

Similarly, prospective secondary science teachers would study the curriculum for which they will be responsible. For example, for science teachers NASDTEC comments:

> The comprehensive science program shall require study designed to assure knowledge of the basic principles of biology, chemistry, physics, and earth and space science and shall require specialization in one of these areas. (p. 73)

In addition to knowing the subject they will teach, teachers must also possess subject matter *to teach with* (Broudy 1972, p. 61). The NCATE *Standards* (1982) say it thusly:

> The professional studies component of each curriculum for prospective teachers includes the study of the content to be taught to pupils, and the supplementary knowledge, from the subject matter of the teaching specialty and from allied fields, that is needed by the teacher for perspective and flexibility in teaching. (p. 17)

For example, secondary school history teachers must know both the history they will teach and history writ large. Additionally, teachers need to know other subjects from which they can draw. Thus history teachers would benefit from study of related literature, music, and art for periods about which they will teach.

The content available in, and supportive of, the teaching specialty seems endless and appears increasingly so. Fortunately, there are criterion measures, albeit subjective, by which the content for the teaching specialty can be better selected: Is this the content that is taught in the schools? Is this the content that will give the curriculum taught in the schools extended or enriched meaning? Is this the content that will help the preservice teacher understand the discipline's attributes and ways of knowing?

Academicians normally teach teachers the content for a teaching specialty and are often referred to as subject matter specialists. They fall into several types. One type is the academician whose major interests are to engage in scholarly research and to nurture others who will go to graduate school and major in the discipline. This type is not interested in teaching the subject specialty in such a way that it meets the needs of K-12 teachers who will teach that specialty to pupils. Howsam et al. (1976) note that since prospective teachers normally populate the same classes as other university students, this raises problems since:

> academic faculty sometimes assume that when . . . education majors learn the research procedures, logic and content of an academic specialty their ability to . . . excite others about the value of the discipline will follow. Some of the faculty also assume that knowledge of a subject is sufficient preparation for teaching it. Courses designed primarily to meet the needs of majors who intend advanced graduate study often neglect the concerns of others, particularly teachers. (pp. 85-86)

A second and related type is the academician who is not particularly interested in scholarship and preparing future graduate students but still treats students as if they all have the same purposes in studying that content area. A third type is the academician who has been given an additional responsibility for teacher preparation and who therefore is sensitive, if not always responsive, to having preservice teachers as students.

There are also persons other than academicians who are knowledgeable and competent to teach the content courses. They may be members of the education faculty or practicing K-12 teachers. Clearly, then, it depends on the motivation of persons teaching prospective teachers their content specialty as to how they will approach the subject matter.

Seaborg and Barzun (1966) comment on the conflict between academicians teaching the content for the teaching specialty and those teaching professional coursework.

> In educating our teachers we had emphasized courses on pedagogy and method to the detriment of preparing them in the subjects they were supposed to teach. . . . There had grown up — regrettably — a rigid estrangement between scientists and science educators, so that science courses for prospective teachers were commonly taught in departments or colleges of education, while professors in the scientific departments often tended to discourage their better students from considering careers as school science teachers. (p. 22)

The situation described above is especially bleak because future teachers need to study their teaching major in special ways. Cogan (1967, p. 110) calls for careful, selective study of the discipline as opposed to extensive coverage; understanding the scope and limitations of the discipline; and development of strategies that enable the teacher to learn how to learn in the discipline. Smith, Cohen, and Pearl (1969) note:

> To be prepared in the subject matter of instruction is to know the content to be taught and how the content can be related to the interests and experience of children and youth. . . . This kind of preparation will require courses oriented to the teacher's need for knowledge that can be tied in with the life of children and youth rather than discipline-oriented courses. (pp. 121-122)

Cogan also reminds us that teachers must develop a "love of learning" for their teaching specialty and must be able to communicate it to pupils. In the final analysis, future teachers need more than knowledge of a discipline. They need to be made to think about how the study of a discipline can make more rational future citizens and how the discipline must be taught in order to do so.

Academicians teaching content courses for teachers would be more sensitive to what preservice teachers need to know if they regularly interacted with K-12 teachers in their specialty area, if they served on school district curriculum committees, or if they interacted with teacher educators in their specialty areas.

Because most academicians teaching content courses for teachers do not maintain relationships with the schools or with teacher educators, they tend to be unaware of or insensitive to the needs of preservice teachers. Therefore, education departments have felt it necessary to establish special methods courses. These courses, to be discussed later, are intended specifically to address both the content and how it should be taught.

A special word needs to be said about the content preparation of elementary teachers since they teach all the common branch subjects. It is assumed that prospective elementary teachers already know the content of the elementary school curriculum because of their general education and that they need no further instruction. Current concerns underlying the teacher competency testing movement deny such an assumption. Some preservice teachers must themselves be taught or retaught the elementary content that they in turn will teach. In such cases, we would generally be hard pressed to find university courses that provide content for or content to support the teaching fields of elementary teachers. An exception would be a course in mathematics, such as Mathematics 105 taught at Ohio State University, which purports "to develop basic ideas of arithmetic, algebra, and geometry as appropriate for elementary school teachers." There are no parallel courses in other academic departments. No like courses exist in science, literature, language arts, or social studies. The existence of this single course seems more of an indictment of the mathematics competency of elementary school teachers than provision of a course intended to enrich or further knowledge of the content specialty.

No one would argue the need for teachers to know their subjects, and criticism is quick to follow those teachers who do not. The challenge for teacher educators is to ensure that teachers "know their stuff."

Contributing to the "content" problem was the transformation of teachers colleges into multipurpose institutions that occurred primarily in the 1940s and 1950s. As a result many different "vocational" majors find themselves in classrooms with academic professors who either do not or cannot cope with the heterogeneity. Thus the same course may be taken by some students as general education, by others as part of their major, and by preservice teachers as content for their teaching specialty.

Following are suggestions that may help to resolve the problems in this area of the professional curriculum:

1. Make the content for teaching specialty courses truly professional courses, rather than placing preservice teachers in courses intended as general education or as prerequisites for graduate study.

2. Define more clearly what should constitute the content for each teaching specialty, focusing on the needs of both elementary and secondary education.

3. Ensure that academicians teaching content for teaching specialty courses are in contact with schools, teachers, and teacher educators.

Humanistic and Behavioral Studies

NCATE (1982) has labeled the second category of professional studies the "humanistic and behavioral studies." It more commonly is referred to as foundations of education or foundational studies in education. Operationally, this component is defined by courses with such diverse titles as introduction to education, philosophy of education, history of education, educational psychology, educational sociology, educational anthropology, politics of education, economics of education, comparative education; and more recently, aesthetic education and moral or ethical education. More than any other component, the humanistic and behavioral studies are intended to serve as bridges between general education and pedagogy. The Philosophy of Education Society (1980) describes them as follows:

> The more *liberal* components of the professional education sequence of teacher education are concerned with the principles, criteria and methods used in making practical judgments in education. These liberalizing professional components focus on clarifying, understanding, justifying and evaluating proposed ends and means in education. Many of the skills and concepts of this component are acquired through humanistic and behavioral studies. . . . Behavioral studies promote understanding of the scientific aspects of practical judgment through the findings and methods of

psychology, sociology, anthropology, economics, and political science. Humanistic studies relate educational concerns to their historical development and to the analytical, interpretive and normative (ethical) perspectives and methods associated with the philosophical study of education. (p. 265)

Thus the intention seems to be to ensure better understanding of education, utilizing knowledge and modes of inquiry from the humanities and social and behavioral sciences.

Several influential sources support including this component in the teacher preparation curriculum. NCATE (1982, p. 17) notes that there are certain issues in education that can be illuminated by considering their historical development and related philosophical, sociological, psychological, political, and religious issues. These issues include the nature and aims of education; the curriculum, organization, and administration of a school system; and the processes of teaching and learning.

The National Association of State Directors of Teacher Education and Certification (1981) expects that:

The beginning teacher shall have completed a program that provides for the development of insights into child and adolescent psychology; the teaching-learning process; the social interactive process in the classroom, school and community . . . the broader problems of the profession as they relate to society and the function of the school. (p. 18)

. . . The program shall require study of the leaders, ideas and movements underlying the development and organization of education in the U.S. (p. 19)

Taylor (1965) feels that humanistic studies help preservice teachers to develop their own philosophical system that can be applied to school. A few argue, as does Conant (1963), that such a component would be unnecessary if only "the general education of future teachers is well arranged." That being the case, "helpful philosophical, political and historical insights will be supplied by professors of philosophy, political science and history" (p. 123). Conant advocates that preservice teachers should "study philosophy under a real philosopher. An additional course in philosophy of education would be desirable but not essential" (1963, p. 131). Broudy strongly disagrees with recommendations like Conant's and argues that such recommendations are not practical.

Even the student who has solid work in philosophy, history, psychology and sociology faces formidable obstacles in determining what in those disciplines is relevant to problems of the curriculum [and so forth]. The professional educator confronted by class after class of students who cannot overcome these obstacles, understandably might do one or two things. He might approach the department of history, philosophy, sociology and psychology with a plea that they design courses that bear more or less directly on his problems or he might try to devise courses of this kind himself. Very often it is the futility of the first approach that makes the second alternative unavoidable. (1963, p. 54)

The Philosophy of Education Society (1980) proposes that faculty teaching humanistic and behavioral studies should hold a doctorate with a major in philosophy of education from a department of philosophy, philosophy of education, or foundations of education, and that at least one faculty member in the department should qualify for a fellowship in the Philosophy of Education Society.

A specific question about humanistic and behavioral studies that needs to be answered is, What knowledge is of most worth? Broudy (1963) argues that we must mold a rational curriculum. He then goes on to remind us that a professional field of study is distinguished by the way it organizes learning around problems distinctive to the profession.

> In this it differs from an intellectual discipline such as mathematics or physics. Mathematics is constituted of an interrelated set of concepts dealing with quantitative relationships. The professional curriculum of the teaching of mathematics . . . organizes materials in terms of teaching and learning mathematics. Such concerns also distinguish education from law, engineering, medicine and other professions. A distinctive set of problems studied in their foundational and specialist dimensions provides the structural framework for any professional field. (p. 50)

Broudy sets forth a taxonomy in which he proposes four problem areas in education that should be studied, including educational aims; the curriculum; school organization, administration, and support; and teaching and learning. The four disciplines that would shed most light on the above problem areas are history, psychology, sociology, and philosophy. It is clear that Broudy's approach, suggested 20 years ago, influenced the NCATE standard for humanistic and behavioral studies (NCATE 1982, p. 17).

Conant (1963), in his study of the education of American teachers, found little semblance of rationality or unity in the content of foundations courses.

> Those in charge of these foundations courses often attempt to patch together scraps of history, philosophy, political theory, sociology and pedagogical ideology. (p. 117)

He referred to them as eclectic courses and advised their elimination, "for not only are they usually worthless, but they give education departments a bad name" (p. 117). What should exist, according to Conant, are:

> Courses in the philosophy, history or sociology of education . . . intended to apply the disciplines of specific academic areas to education. But these too may be of limited value. (p. 127)

Howsam et al. (1976) also find fault with the content and teaching of such courses, but on other grounds. They argue that "Foundations courses are taught as separate disciplines in such a way that students fail to see the interplay between theory and practice" (p. 187). Howsam and his colleagues recommend:

> That a series of changes be made in the formats, conceptual frameworks and delivery modes. . . . To support and strengthen teachers, [they] must become interdisciplinary; unifying in concept and practice; less obscure and more human service functional; problem-based, featuring "theory in practice" modes of inquiry; original and bold in developing explanatory hypotheses; personal and clarifying in terms of beliefs and values; socially activistic and mission centered; and experimental in teaching procedures and delivery modes. (p. 88)

Many preservice teachers do not seem to respond positively to the content of this component. They consider it irrelevant because they can neither relate the knowledge to their experience as learners nor see its usefulness to their future as teachers. The most striking criticism leveled at teachers of the humanities and behavioral studies are that they must become more involved with education practice. Howsam (1976) notes:

> Foundations professors refuse to become involved with field experiences and the problems of practitioners which they perceive as outside the analytic or descriptive function of the discipline. (p. 87)

Compared with other teacher educators, the role of foundations professors is particularly difficult. If they have been prepared well in their disciplines, they are naturally enthusiastic about their respective fields. But many education students do not share that enthusiasm and fail to see how the content relates to the problems of classroom teaching, which they expect their professional courses to cover. Broudy (1963) describes what he believes the humanistic and behavioral studies can and cannot do.

> The sociology or even the psychology of education, for example, will not directly help the second-grade teacher to manage her slow learners. . . . Although foundational knowledge does not solve problems, it does prevent our being naive and provincial about them. (p. 53)

In summary, the humanistic and behavioral studies "properly studied" would result in a teacher who, among other things, would be more able to understand education as a complex activity. Students of such studies would see things in a broader perspective and would continuously be able to value the worth of current practice and ideas.

Although there is general support for the inclusion of foundations courses in the preservice curriculum, it is readily apparent both from practice and from the literature that significant problems persist. Following are some suggestions that may be useful:

1. Identify the concepts from the several foundations areas, individu-

ally and collectively, that would help to illuminate thought and practice in education.

2. Gain consensus from teacher educators and practicing teachers on the appropriateness of teaching these concepts and understandings in the preservice curriculum.

3. Determine when, where, and how the knowledge can best be attained.

4. Ensure that members of the foundations of education faculty acknowledge and support the above determination.

5. When hiring foundations professors, ensure that they primarily are committed to the education of teachers.

6. Reward foundations professors who make such commitments and perform their roles well.

7. Ensure that preservice teachers have an adequate general education that will prepare them for foundational studies.

Teaching and Learning Theory

The third category of professional studies is labeled "teaching and learning theory." This component is legitimized by the NCATE *Standards* (1982) as follows:

> The professional studies component of each curriculum includes the systematic study of teaching and learning theory. (p. 18)

Theory, as used here, means an attempt to provide understanding of the concepts, definitions, facts, and conditional propositions that convey what is known about teaching and learning.

Sources of such teaching and learning theory include professional wisdom gained through teaching experience, knowledge obtained from the social and behavioral sciences, knowledge generated within teacher education units, and knowledge derived from the study of K-12 teaching. Historically, professional wisdom has dominated the content of this component and frequently has been inseparable from advocacy and commitment (Dunkin and Biddle 1974). Teacher educators, for the most part former classroom teachers themselves, frequently draw from their personal knowledge and experience. Call this craft knowledge. Curriculum projects that teacher educators work on reflect this propensity. For example, use of professional wisdom dominated decisions about pedagogical curriculum generally, and teaching and learning theory specifically, when teacher educators worked on the federally sponsored Comprehensive Elementary Teacher Education Models program (CETEM), an effort to redesign the preservice curriculum for elementary teachers (Cruickshank 1970), which is described in Part II.

Later efforts to generate competency-based teacher education (described in Part II) and so-called generic teaching competencies also relied heavily on craft knowledge, although they also used knowledge from the undergirding disciplines and knowledge generated from within teacher education units (Bureau of Academic Programs 1978; Dick, Watson, and Kaufman 1981; Dodl et al. 1971).

Professional organizations that influence the teacher education curriculum also tend to be overly dependent on use of craft knowledge. For example, the NEA publication *Excellence in Our Schools: Teacher Education* (1982) (described in Part II), presents "views of the united teaching profession about needed changes in teacher education." It describes three major functions of the teacher — facilitating learning, managing the classroom, and making professional decisions. From these three major functions of teaching are derived learnings, skills, and field-based experiences. According to NEA, the total document "reflects substantial input by NEA members and represents what practitioners know."

However, efforts are being made to build the content of teaching and learning theory on knowledge derived from studying teaching and learning in natural classrooms. Smith (1983) contends that whereas historically academic disciplines like philosophy and psychology were thought to be the wellsprings of knowledge about teaching and learning, teacher educators increasingly are turning to the accumulating body of "clinical knowledge." According to Smith, we are just coming to see that:

> there is just as much intellectual challenge in mastering, for example, the concept of "praise," the various ways and conditions of using it, and learning to perform in the classroom according to the rules governing the use of praise as there is in the mastery of a particular concept or principle of philosophy or psychology. (pp. 7-8)

As discoveries continue to be made that provide increasing clinical knowledge, it becomes the task of the academic theoretician to provide explanations. For example, why are the effects of praise discrepant? As clinical knowledge increases, educational psychologists or philosophers will be held in higher regard if they can, in fact, provide explanations so that preservice teachers will understand *why* and *how* what they do affects the outcomes.

General and Special Methods Courses. Coursework offered under the teaching and learning theory rubric often is labeled or referred to as "general and special methods." Conant (1963) refers to them as "those terrible methods courses which waste students' time" (p. 137). A general methods course intends to convey what is known about the art and science of teaching that is of common interest and use to K-12 teachers. Conant (1963) notes that a "general methods course assumes the existence of a body of predictive generalizations valid wherever a teaching-learning situation exists" (p. 138). Special methods courses, on the other hand, address that which supposedly is different about teaching various grade levels or content specialties, for example, the teaching of art in first grade as opposed to the teaching of physics in senior high.

26

In the earlier "Content for the Teaching Specialty" section, it was mentioned that there is little opportunity for and frequently little effort made by academicians to tailor their courses for persons who will teach their subject matter in K-12 classrooms. To overcome this shortcoming, teacher education institutions offer a variety of special methods courses. Elementary teacher education, due to its broad curricular responsibilities, is rife with such courses labeled "The Teaching of Art," "The Teaching of Health and Physical Education," "Elementary Social Studies Methods," "Reading in the Elementary School," and so on. As with Conant, many academicians and some of the general public believe these courses to be unnecessary and devoid of intellectual content. Thus, this segment of the professional curriculum is under frequent attack. The defenders, as Gutek (1970) points out, "contend that [they] provide the most practical preparation for elementary school teaching" (p. 140). Generally speaking, special methods courses are offered to ensure that prospective teachers know the curriculum to be taught and how best to present it to K-12 pupils.

Teaching Theory. What should preservice teachers know about teaching to facilitate their work? What should be included in teaching theory courses? John Goodlad notes in "A Study of Schooling" (1983) that:

> At all levels of schooling, a very few teaching procedures — explaining or lecturing, monitoring seatwork, and quizzing — accounted for most of those we observed overall in our sample of 1,016 classrooms. Teachers varied in the quality of their lecturing, for example, but "teacher talk" was by far the dominant classroom activity. (p. 552)

If this indeed is the case, teacher education has the responsibility to ensure that teachers do these things well, that is, explaining, lecturing, monitoring, quizzing. And it would seem appropriate that these skills be at least a part of the study of teaching theory.

The National Education Association (1982) long has argued that preservice teachers should be taught so that they can "start their careers with a background of experiences that allows them to handle classroom situations comfortably" (p. 7). As noted earlier, according to the NEA report *Excellence in Our Schools*, teachers must be prepared to perform three critical functions: 1) facilitating learning, or knowing the unique characteristics of students; 2) managing the classroom, or organizing the classroom to stimulate learning and foster discipline; and 3) making professional decisions such as deciding what to teach. These three functions are elaborated further into learnings, skills, and field-based experiences that are intended to guide teacher preparation institutions in curriculum appraisal and reorganization.

AACTE suggests curricula for teacher education generally, and teaching and learning theory specifically, in Howsam et al. (1976) and Scannell et al. (1982). The Howsam et al. publication calls for the development in teachers of "a broad repertoire of classroom behaviors and skills, grounded in professional and academic knowledge" (p. 88). The requisite behaviors and skills described are similar to a set of 33 used in the preservice curriculum at the University of Houston. They are subsumed under 11 categories: 1) diagnosis and evaluation, 2) organizing the classroom, 3) goals and objectives, 4) planning, 5) communicating, 6) instructing, 7) managing, 8) interpersonal relations, 9) evaluation, 10) self-improvement, and 11) colleagues and other professionals (pp. 160-161).

The Scannell et al. publication extends the suggestions contained in Howsam et al. and speaks to generic teaching knowledge and skills and specialized pedagogical knowledge and skills. The generic teaching knowledge and skills are arranged under eight teacher functions: 1) analyzing and interpreting student abilities, 2) designing instruction to meet learner needs, 3) conducting instruction, 4) managing the classroom, 5) managing student conduct, 6) promoting classroom communication, 7) evaluating learning, and 8) arranging for conferral and referral opportunities.

Smith et al. (1969) note:

> Teachers fail because they have not been trained calmly to analyze . . .
> situations against a firm background of relevant theory. . . . If the
> teacher is incapable of understanding classroom situations, the actions he
> takes will often increase his difficulties. (pp. 28-29)

If this assertion is correct, then it is incumbent upon those preparing preservice teachers to provide them with opportunities to reflect on significant teaching situations and problems and to help them to draw on related theory to analyze and understand the situations (Cruickshank et al. 1980).

More recently, Smith (n.d.) proposes as a starting point a professional curriculum that derives from analysis of the teacher's work: planning, teaching or instructing, classroom control (an area of teacher problems), and evaluation.

Stratemeyer (Cottrell 1956, p. 150) also proposes that the units of instruction in the teacher education curriculum be based on teaching situations and educational problems preservice teachers would encounter. These would include how to become acquainted with students and understand them, how to guide them in developing specific skills, how to evaluate effectively, how to work cooperatively with parents and colleagues, and how to bring about educational change.

One of the most intensive efforts to incorporate theory into the preservice curriculum was undertaken by the Teacher Education and Media (TEAM) project (LaGrone 1964). This project outlines five courses related to teaching and learning theory. Three seem to fit the definition of teaching theory: "The Analytic Study of Teaching," "Design for Teaching-Learning," and "Evaluation of Teaching Competencies." These courses and related others are described in Part II.

A number of theories or models present holistic conceptions of teaching. Sixteen conceptions are described by Joyce and Weil (1972). The work of

Flanders (1970) also provides considerable insight into how teachers teach. The psychology of teaching method is the subject of a National Society for the Study of Education Yearbook (1976).

Most recently, coursework in teaching theory has begun to take note of the research on schooling and especially research on teaching. Consequently, teaching theory increasingly gives attention to topics such as teacher expectancy (Brophy 1983), direct instruction (Good 1979; Rosenshine and Berliner 1978), large-group instruction (Medley 1977), and teacher clarity (Cruickshank, Kennedy, Bush, and Myers 1979; Rosenshine and Furst 1971).

Learning Theory. Preservice students' exposure to learning theory is minimal in most teacher education curricula. When it is offered, it is usually included as part of a course in general psychology or educational psychology. However, there are a number of models that present holistic conceptions of student learning in classroom settings. They include Bennett (1978), Bloom (1976), Bruner (1966), Glaser (1976), and Harnischfeger and Wiley (1976); and they are reviewed elsewhere (Haertel, Walberg, and Weinstein 1983). The knowledge about learning and teaching contained in these writings fits comfortably into the learning theory requirement.

Conant (1963) argues that the content of teaching and learning theory and general methods classes is basically the same as the content taught in courses in general psychology and educational psychology, and he concludes that they are "unnecessary duplication." His judgment of special methods courses is equally negative. If particular knowledge or skills are needed, he feels, they can best be learned as part of the practicum (p. 138). Also, Conant eschews methods courses because there is no agreement on a common body of knowledge that all teachers should have before taking their first full-time job (p. 141).

The following suggestions are offered to improve the teaching and learning theory component of the preservice curriculum:

1. Sustained efforts should be undertaken to collect and codify teaching and learning theory from a variety of sources. The result could be a manual that provides concise but authoritative references for teacher educators (and practicing teachers). Such a manual would be similar to the desk references used by physicians and veterinarians.

2. In the interim, the content for teaching and learning theory courses should be selected, to the extent possible, on the basis of empirically verified findings, rather than on personal opinions or preferences.

3. Those who teach special methods courses in their subject areas should keep in mind the differences between general and special methods. Special methods courses are designed to ensure that preservice teachers know the K-12 curriculum they will teach and the special approaches or alternative ways of teaching it.

4. Agreement must be reached on the content of teaching and learning theory courses in order to eliminate unnecessary duplication of topics.

5. Greater attention should be given to teachers learning problem-solving skills and the related theory in addressing classroom problems.

6. Whether learning theory is taught in educational psychology or in some other course, it must be a highly visible component in the preservice professional curriculum.

7. Those who teach teaching and learning theory are the glue that holds the professional program together. These persons, above all others, need a broad understanding of the whole preservice curriculum and the role that teaching and learning theory plays therein.

Laboratory, Clinical, and Practicum Experiences

A final component of professional studies consists of teaching experiences in natural classrooms or in contrived settings. The purpose of these experiences is to provide preservice teachers with work or worklike settings in which they may study teaching and put to use what they already have learned about teaching and learning. The field or school-based experiences include: *observations*, where preservice teachers observe but do not themselves engage in real teaching; part-time *participation*, where engagement in real teaching is limited to trying out selected teaching abilities (for example, leading a small-group discussion) following procedures learned in teaching theory classes; part-time *apprenticeships*, where preservice teachers learn by practical experience under the guidance of skilled teachers; and finally full-time *practicum* or student teaching, where preservice teachers work in a classroom for an extended period of time and are expected to assume most, if not all, responsibility for teaching.

The contrived and scaled-down teaching experiences, undertaken on campus, include: *peer teaching*; *mirror teaching*, which merely is video recording of peer teaching; and *microteaching*, which is video recording of teaching peers any of 18 or more specific teaching skills (Allen and Ryan 1969). Other experiences of this type are *simulations*, where, for example, preservice teachers take on the role of a teacher in order to resolve common teaching concerns or problems (Cruickshank, Broadbent, and Bubb 1967; Cruickshank 1969); and *Reflective Teaching*, where preservice teachers teach brief, standardized lessons to peers, are given feedback by peers regarding their skill in presenting the lessons, and then reflect on the teaching they have done (Cruickshank, Holton, Fay, Williams, Kennedy, Myers, and Hough 1981). Still another type of simulated experience is the use of *protocol materials*, where, for example, preservice teachers view a videotape of a significant event in a classroom and then are provided with related theoretical knowledge that illuminates the event (Smith et al. 1969). These various forms of on-campus experience are discussed more fully in Part III.

Thus preservice teachers can have direct experience with reality in regular classrooms, but they also can have direct experiences with *models of reality* in contrived, simulated settings. Both types of experiences can be categorized as laboratory or clinical. Lindsey (1971) describes a laboratory experience as:

> a place for the systematic study of teaching — a place where a student may discover what teaching is and how the many and diverse variables in a complex teaching-learning environment interact with each other. It is a place where a prospective teacher may test his knowledge about teaching and verify or modify his understanding of that knowledge. (p. 84)

Under Lindsey's definition, all of the school-based and on-campus activities could quality as laboratory experiences. However, in practice, many fall short. Student teaching is a good example. While it has the necessary conditions to become a laboratory activity, it frequently is not, since student teachers are not truly viewed and treated as students of teaching involved in discovering, testing, reflecting, modifying, and so forth. Rather, too often student teaching is characterized best as learning to cook at mother's side in the kitchen or modeling the master.

Clinical experience is the term reserved for situations in which preservice teachers actually analyze and treat learners in a manner similar to that of physicians who diagnose and prescribe to patients. To be considered clinical experience in preservice teaching, Mills (n.d.) requires that, among other things, the activity must present a case or problem — either simulated or real — that relates directly to school-aged children and youth; provide opportunity for the preservice teacher to study and practice analytic, diagnostic, and prescriptive skills; and provide systematic feedback to assist the preservice teacher in developing and improving performance (p. 9).

Laboratory, clinical, and practicum experiences have been included in the curriculum at least since the early nineteenth century. At the Normal School at Lexington, Massachusetts, Peirce (1926) mentioned such experiences for his preservice teachers:

> by requiring my pupils to teach each other in my presence . . . and . . . by means of the Model School, where under my supervision, the normal pupils had an opportunity, both to prove and improve their skills in teaching and managing schools. (pp. 279-280)

At about the same time, Edwards (1865) wrote:

> Another essential requisite in a normal school is, that it gives its pupils an opportunity of some kind of practice in teaching, under the supervision and subject to the criticism of experienced and skillful instructors. This is accomplished in various ways: by exercises in conducting the regular classes of the Normal School; by classes of normal pupils assuming for the time the character of children and receiving instructions and answering questions as they think children would; and by a separate school of children in which the novice is instructed with the charge of a class, either permanently or for a stated period. (p. 280)

31

More recently, laboratory, clinical, and practicum experiences have been advocated by the Commission on Teacher Education (1946) and by Conant (1963), who describes laboratory experience positively as follows:

> Let me return now to the term "laboratory experience," which refers to both the observation of children and the practical activity in the classroom carried on in conjunction with professional instruction . . . it seems clear that the future . . . teacher has much to learn that can be learned only in the . . . classroom. . . . I would argue that all education courses for elementary teachers . . . be accompanied by "laboratory experiences" providing for the observation and teaching of children. To some extent limited use of film and television can take the place of direct classroom observation. (p. 161)

Additionally, Conant recommends most emphatically that all elementary and secondary teachers should engage in "practice teaching."

Clark, Snow, and Shavelson (1976) make a strong case for specific laboratory experiences when they summarize three studies on learning to teach.

> Practice, by itself, did not enable teachers to increase student achievement. This finding indicates that teachers might profit from a process that would enable them to observe more systematically the effects of their teaching on students — i.e., a training program that would help teachers become researchers of their own teaching effectiveness. (p. 180)

The American Association of Colleges for Teacher Education teacher education curriculum study (Scannell et al. 1983) supports laboratory, clinical, and practicum experiences by calling for "a series of carefully designed and supervised campus- and field-based experiences . . . conducted throughout the period of professional study" (p. 15). The experiences should include "simulations and other controlled situations, Microteaching, Reflective Teaching, observation of teachers, and student teaching." Clearly, there seems to be no lack of interest in and support for this preservice curriculum component.

Issues Related to Laboratory, Clinical, and Practicum Experiences

One of the issues associated with laboratory, clinical, and practicum experiences is how they should be sequenced and how one relates to the other. According to Nolan (1982):

> Our failure to be cognizant of the distinction in terminology between early professional laboratory experiences and practicum experiences . . . has resulted in a professional viewpoint which sees the purpose of student teaching as the development of teaching skills which were practiced previously in earlier field experiences . . . [whereas] the purpose of student teaching [is] a continuation of the scientific inquiry, hypothesis testing and experimentation which were first practiced in the relatively safe environment of early laboratory experiences. (p. 52)

He argues, like Dewey (1904), that laboratory experiences should occur before student teaching, and that "they should be designed to foster *reflective criticism* of the methods of instruction and the purposes of education and enable the preservice teacher to be a more thoughtful and alert student of teaching" (p. 49). Therefore, "the apprenticeship" should occur only after the preservice teacher has developed the methods of reflective inquiry. Nolan would agree that more on-campus laboratory experiences, such as Reflective Teaching, simulations, or protocol materials, are a necessary but missing link between classroom theory and the practicum.

A related problem associated with laboratory, clinical, and practicum experiences is the failure to make these experiences laboratory-like as defined by Lindsey (1971). Lindsey's definition of laboratory experiences contained explicit concepts such as "systematic study of teaching," "discover . . . how the many and diverse variables in a complex teaching-learning environment interact," "testing and verifying knowledge of teaching," and so forth. It also implied practice with feedback.

Howsam et al. (1976) address the concept of laboratory experiences in the context of the teacher education classroom:

> The teacher education classroom should be a laboratory for the study and development of teaching knowledge and skills. This laboratory should be expanded to include instructional procedures such as microteaching, simulation, modeling and demonstration. These procedures help students to confront a controlled reality by concentrating on particular teaching-learning behaviors until they attain adequate levels of skills and confidence. When students do encounter the complexity of a regular classroom, they will have experienced a planned series of teaching acts in a minimally threatening environment, with immediate feedback and experienced supervision (p. 93)

With both Lindsey and Howsam, we have operational definitions of what ideal laboratory teaching experiences should be like. In practice the reality falls short of the ideal.

A problem associated with clinical experience is the failure to provide such opportunities. This is partly because the concept of clinical experiences is not fully understood and partly because they require special settings and materials and generous amounts of time.

In practice, there have been few opportunities for the preservice teacher in the field or on campus actually to engage in diagnostic and prescriptive activities and to receive systematic feedback, which are the essence of the clinical approach. Furthermore, clinical experience has not been a required part of preservice programs for long, because teacher educators have tended to rely on craft knowledge or common sense and on knowledge from such disciplines as psychology and sociology. Smith (1983) contends that reliance on academic knowledge for use in clinical situations is inadequate because we cannot deduce effective teaching from what is gleaned from another discipline. Rather, he argues that we must study effective teaching in its own right in order to discover professional content that can be applied to clinical experience. The more we study teaching and learning in the classroom, the more we will accumulate knowledge that has a direct relationship to teaching practice. Providing what Smith terms "clinical knowledge" may well be the impetus needed for improvement of clinical experiences.

Who controls field experiences has long been an issue in the preservice curriculum. The primary responsibility has tended to rest with the teacher education programs in colleges and universities that have been approved by their respective state departments of education. However, local school districts also have vested interests since they provide the workplace. The issue of control arises when the workplace is selected, cooperating teachers are chosen, the role of the preservice teacher is defined, conferencing is done, and preservice teachers are evaluated.

A major problem associated with the practicum experience is enhancing its image among teacher educators and academicians. As long as it continues to be viewed simply as an apprenticeship, it will be shunned by those who view their professional role as more important than just monitoring behavior. As the practicum experience becomes more laboratory and clinically oriented, its image probably will improve.

A further problem associated with practicum experiences has been the failure to use the research on teaching and school effectiveness. As the results of such research accumulate and are validated, it is encumbent on practicum supervisors to ensure that preservice teachers can apply what is known, for example, about "clarity" (Cruickshank, Kennedy, Bush, and Myers 1979), "time on task" (Carrol 1963), "with-it-ness" (Dunkin and Biddle 1974), and so forth.

Some of the other continuing issues associated with field experiences are suggested by McIntyre (1983) in the form of the following questions:

1. What should be learned from field experience?
2. How valid are current types of field experiences? What effects do they have?
3. What are the roles and relationships of preservice teachers, cooperating teachers, and university supervisors? How can persons be better prepared for these roles?
4. How should field experiences be structured?
5. How can field experiences be made more like laboratory experiences in order to foster inquiry and reflection rather than being merely an apprenticeship experience?
6. How should preservice teacher performance in the field be evaluated?

Suggestions for improving the laboratory, clinical, and practicum component of the preservice curriculum are:

1. Obtain consensus regarding the outcomes of field experiences (apprenticeships, observation, participation, practicum).
2. Determine to what extent the various field experiences are valid for each outcome.
3. Gain consensus on the roles and relationships of persons involved in field experiences.
4. Determine how best to prepare each subgroup for its role and do so.
5. Gain consensus on how the variety of field experiences should be structured and when they should be presented.
6. Investigate how pure field experiences can be transformed into more professionally meaningful laboratory and clinical experiences and do so.
7. Reach agreement on how preservice teachers should be evaluated during field experiences.
8. Support the identification and verification of knowledge that can be used to enhance clinical experience.
9. Obtain consensus regarding the outcomes of on-campus laboratory experiences.
10. Determine to what extent different kinds of on-campus laboratory experiences — simulations, microteaching, Reflective Teaching — are valid for each outcome.
11. Determine the place and sequence for on-campus laboratory experiences.
12. Support development and use of true forms of on-campus laboratory experiences.
13. Obtain consensus on how preservice teachers should be evaluated during on-campus laboratory experiences.

Summary Recommendations

As this century draws to a close, it seems an appropriate time to think about the current curriculum for educating teachers so that as issues and problems emerge recommendations are forthcoming. So far, the curriculum and the issues and problems attendant to it have been presented. Following are some overall suggestions for action by interested parties in addition to those noted throughout Part I.

1. A permanent national teacher education curriculum council should be formed. This council should be nurtured by the National Association of State Directors of Teacher Education and Certification (NASDTEC), since teacher education is, by law, primarily a function of the states and NASDTEC represents state education department program approval and certification

agencies. Support for such a council should come initially from a foundation, but the costs ultimately should be borne by the states through their education departments. The council should represent all parties responsible for and interested in teacher preparation including teacher organizations, colleges and universities, local education agencies, teacher education associations, accrediting and extraordinary approval agencies, the federal government, and philanthropic foundations. The purpose of the council would be to ensure that the curriculum for teacher education is valid. In so doing, it would address general and specific issues and problems related to teacher preparation curricula and would commission inquiries and papers; and it generally would act as a force to better preservice programs.

2. The role of the teacher should be better defined so that the preservice curriculum can be designed to prepare persons for that role. Role definitions for a teacher are practically non-existent. NCATE *Standards* (1982) call for role definitions, yet fail to provide one. With a precise description of what a teacher does, a curriculum can be developed that is both efficient and effective.

3. The numerous teacher education curricula developed over the past century should be identified, organized, analyzed, and presented in such a way that they become a legacy from which to draw.

4. Teacher education scholars and organizations should give attention to recurrent issues and problems in the teacher education curriculum in an effort to resolve them.

5. Teacher education institutions should take the initiative for continuing revision of the curriculum, and not wait for intermittent accreditation or program approval team visits to give impetus to change.

6. Models for teacher education curriculum development should be identified, organized, and presented in such a way that they become a resource from which to draw.

7. Inquiry in teacher education should be encouraged and rewarded so that an expanded knowledge base is available to undergird the teacher education curriculum.

8. The concept of general education for teachers should be explored in order to determine how and how well teachers currently are being educated.

9. Validated clinical knowledge about teaching and learning should be aggregated in such a way that it can be made available to preservice teachers. Such knowledge would be published in a manual or reference similar to the desk references available to physicians and veterinarians. This manual or reference would be a basic reference for preservice teachers.

10. The best time sequence for the teacher education curriculum should be determined by comparing results of its placement throughout a four-year program, as an upper undergraduate level program, or as a graduate, fifth-year program.

11. A determination should be made as to what part of the curriculum can

36

be best taught on campus and what can be best taught in the field.

12. Teacher educators should be required as part of their preparation to study the whole of the teacher education curriculum and its attendant issues and problems.

References for Part I

Adler, M. *The Paideia Proposal: An Educational Manifesto.* New York: Macmillan, 1982.

Allen, D., and Ryan, K. *Microteaching.* Reading, Mass.: Addison-Wesley, 1969.

American Association of Colleges for Teacher Education. *Task Force on Extended Programs Report.* Washington, D.C., 1982.

Armstrong, W.E. "The Teacher Education Curriculum." *Journal of Teacher Education* 8 (1957): 1-16.

Bennett, S.N. "Recent Research on Teaching: A Dream, a Belief, and a Model," *British Journal of Educational Psychology* 48 (1978): 127-47.

Bloom, B.S. *Human Characteristics and School Learning.* New York: McGraw-Hill, 1976.

Borrowman, M.L., ed. *Teacher Education in America.* New York: Teachers College Press, 1966.

Boyer, E.L., and Levine, A. *A Quest for Common Learning: The Aims of General Education.* Washington, D.C.: The Carnegie Foundation for the Advancement of Teaching, 1981.

Brophy, J. *Research on the Self-Fulfilling Prophecy and Teacher Expectations.* Institute for Research on Teaching Research Series No. 119. East Lansing: IRT, Michigan State University, 1983.

Broudy, H.S. *The Real World of the Public School.* New York: Harcourt, Brace & Jovanovich, 1972.

Broudy, H.S. *The Scholars and the Public Schools.* Columbus: Ohio State University Press, 1963.

Bruner, J.S. *Toward a Theory of Instruction.* New York: Norton, 1966.

Bureau of Academic Programs. *More from Performance and Competency Based Teacher Education: Inventories of Specialized Competencies.* Harrisburg: Pennsylvania Department of Education, Office of Higher Education, 1978.

Carroll, J.B. "A Model of School Learning." *Teachers College Record* 64 (1963): 723-33.

Chandler, B.J.; Powell, D.; and Hazzard, W. *Education and the New Teacher.* New York: Dodd, Mead & Co., 1971.

Clark. M.C.; Snow, R.; and Shavelson, R. "Three Experiments on Learning to Teach." *Journal of Teacher Education* 27, no. 2 (1976): 174-79.

Cogan, M. L. "The Academic Major in the Education of Teachers." In *Improving Teacher Education in the United States,* edited by Stanley Elam. Bloomington, Ind.: Phi Delta Kappa, 1967.

Commission on Teacher Education. *The Improvement of Teacher Education: A Final Report by the Commission on Teacher Education.* Washington, D.C.: American Council on Education, 1946.

Conant, J. *The Education of American Teachers.* New York: McGraw-Hill, 1963.

Cooley, W.W., and Leinhardt, G. *The Application of a Model for Investigating Classroom Processes.* Pittsburgh, Pa.: University of Pittsburgh, Learning Research and Development Center, 1975.

Cottrell, D.P., ed. *Teacher Education for a Free People.* Washington, D.C.: American Association of Colleges for Teacher Education, 1956.

Cruickshank, D.R. *Forces Affecting Preservice Teacher Education: Toward an Informed Body Politic of Teacher Educators.* Columbus: Ohio State University Press, 1983.

Cruickshank, D.R. *Blueprints for Teacher Education: A Review of Phase II Proposals for the USDE Comprehensive Elementary Teacher Education (CETEM) Program.* Washington, D.C.: U.S. Department of Health, Education and Welfare, 1970.

Cruickshank, D.R. *The Inner-City Simulation Laboratory.* Chicago: Science Research Associates, 1969.

Cruickshank, D.R.; Applegate, J.; Holton, J.; Mager, J.; Myers, B.; Novak, C.; and Tracey, K. *Teaching Is Tough.* Englewood Cliffs, N.J.: Prentice-Hall, 1980.

Cruickshank, D.R.; Broadbent, F.; and Bubb, R. *The Teaching Problems Laboratory.* Chicago: Science Research Associates, 1967.

Cruickshank, D.R.; Holton, J.; Fay, D.; Williams, J.; Kennedy, J.; Myers, B.; and Hough, B. *Reflective Teaching.* Bloomington, Ind.: Phi Delta Kappa, 1981.

Cruickshank, D.R.; Kennedy, J.; Bush, A.; and Myers, B. "Clear Teaching: What Is It?" *British Journal of Teacher Education* 5 (1979): 27-33.

Cruickshank, D.R., and Thompson, L. "Do We Educate Teachers for a Patchwork Curriculum?" *Educational Leadership* 36 (1978): 127-30.

Department of Education. *Florida Teacher Certification Examination.* Tallahassee: State of Florida Department of Education on Teacher Certification Section, 1982.

Dewey, J. *Democracy and Education.* New York: Macmillan, 1916.

Dewey, J. "The Relationship of Theory to Practice in Education." In *Teacher Education in America: A Documentary History,* edited by M.L. Borrowman. New York: Teachers College Press, 1965. (Originally published in 1904)

Dick, W.; Watson, K.; and Kaufman, R. "Deriving Competencies: Consensus Versus Model Building." *Educational Research* 10 (1981): 5-10.

Dodl, N.; Elfner, E.; Becker, J.; Halstead, J.; Jung, H.; Nelson, P.; Purinton, S.; and Wegele, P. *Florida Catalog of Teacher Competencies.* Tallahassee: Florida State University, 1972.

Dunkin, M., and Biddle, B. *The Study of Teaching.* New York: Holt, Rinehart & Winston, 1974.

Edwards, R. "Normal Schools in the United States." In *Lectures and Proceedings,* National Teachers Association, 1865.

Flanders, N.A. *Analyzing Teacher Behavior.* Reading, Mass.: Addison-Wesley, 1970.

Florida Beginning Teacher Program. *Handbook of the Florida Performance Measurement System.* Tallahassee, Fla.: Office of Teacher Education, Certification and Inservice Staff Development, 1983.

Gagne, R.M. *Essentials of Learning and Instruction.* Hinsdale, Ill.: Dryden Press, 1974.

Glaser, R. "Components of a Psychology of Instruction: Toward a Science of Design." *Review of Educational Research* 46 (1976): 1-24.

Good, T. "Teacher Effectiveness in the Elementary School." *Journal of Teacher Education* 30, no. 2 (1979): 52-64.

Goodlad, J.I. *A Place Called School.* New York: McGraw-Hill, 1983.

Goodlad, J.I. "A Study of Schooling: Some Implications for School Improvement." *Phi Delta Kappan* 64 (April 1983): 552-58.

Gubser, L. Personal communication. 20 November 1982.

Gutek, G.L. *An Historical Introduction to American Education.* New York: Harper and Row, 1970.

Haertel, G.D.; Walberg, H.J.; and Weinstein, T. "Psychological Models of Educational Performance: A Theoretical Synthesis of Constructs." *Review of Educational Research* 53 (1983): 75-91.

Handy, R., and Harwood, E.C. *A Current Appraisal of the Behavioral Sciences.* Great Barrington, Mass.: Behavioral Research Council, 1973.

Harnischfeger, A., and Wiley, D. "The Teaching Learning Process in Elementary Schools: A Synoptic View." *Curriculum Inquiry* 6 (1976): 5-43.

Harvard Committee on General Education. *General Education in a Free Society.* Cambridge, Mass., 1945.

"Help! Teachers Can't Teach." *Time,* 16 June 1980, pp. 54-63.

Howsam, R.B. "The Workplace: Does It Hamper Professionalization of Pedagogy?" *Phi Delta Kappan* 62 (October 1980): 93-96.

Howsam, R.B.; Corrigan, D.; Denemark, G.; and Nash, R. *Educating a Profession.* Washington, D.C.: American Association of Colleges for Teacher Education, 1976.

Joyce, B., and Weil, M. *Models of Teaching.* Englewood Cliffs, N.J.: Prentice-Hall, 1972.

Koerner, J. *The Miseducation of American Teachers.* Boston: Houghton Mifflin, 1963.

LaGrone, H. *A Proposal for the Revision of the Pre-service Professional Component of a Program of Teacher Education.* Washington, D.C.: American Association of Colleges for Teacher Education, 1964.

Lindsey, M. "Teachers, Education of: Laboratory Experiences." In *The Encyclopedia of Education.* New York: Macmillan, The Free Press, 1971.

McIntyre, D.J. *Field Experiences in Teacher Education.* Washington, D.C.: Foundation for Excellence in Teacher Education and the ERIC Clearinghouse on Teacher Education, 1983.

Medley, D. *Teacher Competence and Teacher Effectiveness.* Washington, D.C.: American Association of Colleges for Teacher Education, 1977.

Mills, P. "Integrating Clinical Experiences Within the Teacher Education Curriculum at Bowling Green State University." In *Clinical Experience in Teacher Education,* edited by J. Gress. Columbus: Ohio Association of Teacher Educators and Ohio Association of Colleges for Teacher Education, n.d.

Nash, P.; Shiman, D.; and Conrad, D. "Can the Foundations of Education Survive? Grappling with Our Death Wish." *Journal of Teacher Education* 28, no. 1 (1977): 4-7.

National Assessment of Educational Progress. *Update on Education: A Digest of the National Assessment of Educational Progress.* Denver, Colo.: Education Commission of the States, 1975.

National Association of State Directors of Teacher Education and Certification. *Standards for State Approval of Teacher Education,* 1981 ed. Salt Lake City: Utah State Office of Education, Staff Development Section, 1981.

National Council for Accreditation of Teacher Education. *Standards for the Accreditation of Teacher Education.* Washington, D.C., 1982.

National Education Association. *Excellence in Our Schools: Teacher Education, an Action Plan.* Washington, D.C., 1982.

National Society for the Study of Education. *The Psychology of Teaching Methods.* Chicago: University of Chicago Press, 1976.

Nolan, J.F. "Professional Laboratory Experiences: The Missing Link in Teacher Education." *Journal of Teacher Education* 33, no. 4 (1983): 49-53.

Ornstein, A.C. "The Trend Toward Increased Professionalism for Teachers." *Phi Delta Kappan* 63 (November 1981): 196-98.

Peirce, C., "The Journals of Cyrus Peirce and Mary Swift." In *The First State Normal School in America,* edited by A.O. Norton. Cambridge, Mass.: Harvard University Press, 1926.

Phenix, P.H. *Realms of Meaning: A Philosophy of the Curriculum for General Education.* New York: McGraw-Hill, 1964.

Philosophy of Education Society. "Standards for Academic and Professional Instruction in Philosophy of Education." *Educational Theory* 30 (1980): 265-68.

Ritsch, F.F. "Teacher Preparation and the Liberal Arts." *Educational Forum* 45 (1981): 405-10.

Rosenshine, B., and Berliner, D. "Academic Engaged Time." *British Journal of Teacher Education* 4, no. 1 (1978): 3-16.

Rosenshine, B., and Furst, N. "Research in Teacher Performance Criteria." In *Research in Teacher Education,* edited by B.O. Smith. Englewood Cliffs, N.J.: Prentice-Hall, 1971.

Sametz, L.; Mcloughlin, C.; and Streb, V. "Legal Education for Preservice Teachers: Basics or Remediation." *Journal of Teacher Education* 34, no. 2 (1983): 10-12.

Scannell, D.P.; Corrigan, D.C.; Denemark, G.; Dieterle, L.; Egbert, R.; and Nielsen, R. *Educating a Profession: Profile of a Beginning Teacher.* Washington, D.C.: American Association of Colleges for Teacher Education, 1983.

Schein, E.H. *Professional Education.* New York: McGraw-Hill, 1972.

Seaborg, G.T., and Barzun, J. *The Sciences and the Humanities in the Schools After a Decade of Reform.* Washington, D.C.: Council for Basic Education, 1966.

Seligman, J., and Malamud, P. "Harvard's Hard Core." *Newsweek,* 15 May 1978, p. 61.

Sewall, G.T. "Against Anomie and Amnesia: What Basic Education Means in the Eighties." *Phi Delta Kappan* 63 (May 1982): 603-606.

Sherwin, S. *Teacher Education: A Status Report.* Princeton, N.J.: Educational Testing Service, 1974.

Silberman, C.E. *Crisis in the Classroom: The Remaking of American Education.* New York: Random House, 1970.

Smith, B.O. "Teacher Education in Transition." Paper presented at the annual meeting of the American Association of Colleges for Teacher Education in Detroit, Mich., February 1983.

Smith, B.O. *Design for a School of Pedagogy.* Washington, D.C.: U.S. Government Printing Office, 1980.

Smith, B.O. "The Liberal Arts and Teacher Education." In *The Liberal Arts and Teacher Education,* edited by D. Bigelow. Lincoln: University of Nebraska Press, 1971.

Smith, B.O. *On the Content of Teacher Education.* Tampa: University of South Florida, n.d.

Smith, B.O.; Cohen, S.B.; and Pearl, A. *Teachers for the Real World.* Washington, D.C.: American Association of Colleges for Teacher Education, 1969.

Smith, P.G. "Teacher Education at the Crossroads." Paper presented at the Boyd H. Bode Memorial Lecture No. 2, Ohio State University College of Education, Columbus, 1974.

Stengel, R. "Quality, Not Just Quantity: The Paideia Proposal Aims to Reform America's Schools." *Time,* 6 September 1982, p. 59.

Task Force to Study Program Leading to Certification for Teachers of Social Studies. *Social Studies Competencies.* Minnesota Department of Education Professions Development Section, Multi-State Consortium on Performanced-based Teacher Education. Reprint. Albany: University of the State of New York, State Education Department, 1973.

Taylor, H. "Philosophy and Education." In *Five Fields and Teacher Education,* edited by D.B. Gowin and C. Richardson. Ithaca, N.Y.: Cornell University, 1965.

Tomko, T.N. "Philosophy of Education: Analysis in Search of a Purpose." *Review of Education* 3 (1977): 287-95.

Verduin, J.R. *Conceptual Models in Teacher Education.* Washington, D.C.: American Association of Colleges for Teacher Education, 1967.

Ward, C. "Teacher Education Admissions Testing." *American Association of Colleges for Teacher Education Briefs* 9 (1981): 4, 5.

Watts, D. "Four Views of NCATE's Role and Function." *Phi Delta Kappan* 64 (May 1983): 646-49.

Weaver, W.T. "In Search of Quality: The Need for Talent in Teaching." *Phi Delta Kappan* 61 (September 1979): 29-32, 46.

Whitehead, A.N. *The Aims of Education.* New York: Mentor Books, 1949.

Winter, D.G.; McClelland, D.C.; and Stewart, A.J. *A New Case for the Liberal Arts.* San Francisco: Jossey-Bass, 1981.

Part II
Alternative Teacher
Education Curricula

Education is beyond repair! What is needed is radical reform. This reform is to include the nature of the schooling process, the systems which control educational policy, and the institutions which prepare persons to be teachers.

Smith, Cohen, and Pearl
Teachers for the Real World
1969, p. 9

Over the years the teacher education curriculum has changed both its character and length. Samuel Hall, a Congregational minister who in 1830 became head of the normal department at Phillips Andover Academy, was perhaps the first American to write about a curriculum for teachers. In his *Lectures to School-Masters on Teaching* (1833), he advocates that teachers be prepared in the "science of education" and stresses that they need to be qualified in the management and government of a school; the teaching of spelling, reading, arithmetic, geography, English grammar, writing, history, and composition; how to gain the attention of students; and how to begin the first day of school, among other qualifications.

The first normal school for teachers was established in Lexington, Massachusetts, in 1839; and others were established soon thereafter in Barre and Bridgewater, Massachusetts. The curriculum offered consisted of reading, writing, grammar, arithmetic, geography, spelling, composition, vocal music, drawing, physiology, algebra, philosophy, methodology, and scriptural reading (Gutek 1970, p. 135). In the Lexington Normal School the first principal, Cyrus Peirce, taught 17 different subjects, supervised a model school of 30 pupils, served as demonstration teacher, developed professional materials, and was the janitor.

Henry Barnard wrote in 1851 that most teacher training institutions in

Massachusetts offered courses in algebra, geometry, astronomy, natural philosophy, intellectual philosophy, natural history, English, English literature, U.S. history, and historical geography.

Despite Samuel Hall's advocacy of a "science of education" in 1833, until the 1870s the teacher preparation curriculum was oriented toward academic subjects, which combined general education with academic content that the prospective teacher ultimately would teach to pupils. However, there was a gradual shift toward education courses and pedagogy. By 1889, Monroe (1952) noted that the typical teacher education curriculum consisted of history of education, principles of teaching, methods in the elementary branches, educational psychology, classroom management, and student teaching.

By 1900 many normal school curricula had been extended to two years and training was available for secondary teachers as well. Gradually, most normal schools evolved into teachers colleges with the transition almost complete by 1948-49. Over this period, programs lengthened from two to three to four years, and a discernible curriculum pattern emerged consisting of a general education component, a sequence of content courses that the teacher eventually would teach, a professional education component covering educational foundations (philosophy, history, psychology), teaching and learning theory, and campus- and field-based teaching experiences. This pattern persists today even after the transformation of teachers colleges into multipurpose colleges and universities.

Following World War II, and particularly since the 1960s, a number of different ideas for teacher education emerged from a variety of sources, including the federal government, private foundations, teacher education and teacher associations, university teacher education units, and interested individuals. All were efforts to overcome the perceived shortcomings of the existing teacher preparation curriculum.

Following is a truncated report on 22 proposals made over the past two decades to reform or improve preservice and inservice education in the United States. They have been aggregated here so that teacher educators might consider how, if at all, they can strengthen the traditional curriculum pattern. The list of proposals is not complete by any means; it consists of those I refer to in my own teaching and generally treats only the parts of these proposals that address preservice curriculum.

1. A Harvard President's Curriculum for Teachers

Former Harvard President James Conant brought the problems of teacher education to the attention of the literate public when his book, *The Education of American Teachers* (1963), reached the best-seller list. Based on a two-year study that took Conant and his staff to 77 colleges and state education offices, the book offered numerous recommendations to state boards of education, state legislatures, local school boards, teacher education institutions, and voluntary accrediting agencies.

In general, Conant suggests that each college or university preparing teachers be permitted to develop whatever program of teacher education it considers best, subject to just two conditions. First, the institution's president, on behalf of the entire faculty, must certify that the candidate is adequately prepared to teach on a specific level or in specific fields. Second, the institution, in conjunction with a public school, must establish a state-approved student-teaching program.

Having said that, Conant gives considerable attention to the general, specialized, and professional education requirements for a bachelor's degree. In terms of general education, he advises that half the students' time for four years be devoted to "broad *academic* education." This would include the continued study of subjects begun in secondary schools: literature, history, government, mathematics, natural sciences, geography, art, and music. Those subjects should be studied until the prospective teacher "has attained enough competence to teach the subject to a 12th-grade average class" (p. 94). He adds courses in foreign language, English ("the nature of the language"), philosophy, sociology, anthropology, economics, political science, and psychology, the last six subjects to be taught at an introductory level. An illustration of a 20-course, 60-semester-hour academic program is presented in chapter 5 of his book (see Figure 1 on page 10). Clearly Conant, like Adler (1982) and Silberman (1970), not only expects that teachers should be generally well educated but also that such education must commence at least in secondary school.

Regarding specialization, or preparation in depth in the subject to be taught, Conant notes:

> Only through pursuing a subject well beyond the introductory level can the student gain a coherent picture of the subject, get a glimpse of the vast reaches of knowledge, feel the cutting edge of disciplined training, and discover the satisfactions of a scholarly habit of mind. (p. 106)

Relatedly, he proposes that prospective English, biology, or mathematics teachers should complete a concentration of at least 12 courses, or somewhat more than a full year of college, in their subject specialty.

When it comes to the question of professional courses in education, Conant suggests four "components of a teacher's intellectual and emotional equipment" plus student teaching. The first he calls the "democratic social component" in which teachers must address the development of proper attitudes in pupils, for example, "future citizens whose actions will assure the survival of our *free* society" (p. 114). The second component would address social behavior in which teachers would learn how social behavior emerges in groups of children and would address such questions as "What kind of social behavior do we want to develop?" The third component would focus on child development more generally. Finally, preservice teachers would study principles of teaching. This last component would focus on helping preservice teachers to learn to do "what good schoolteachers do." These tasks include: selecting and organizing instructional materials, presenting information in a form understandable by the young, working with diverse pupils, maintaining discipline, developing interests in fields of study, reporting to parents and the community, and justifying or changing the school's efforts and curriculum.

More specifically, Conant proposes a model of 30 semester hours of coursework for elementary preservice teachers including: child growth and development; a course in history, philosophy, or sociology of education; courses in teaching reading; workshops on the content and methods of elementary school subjects; and year-long laboratory experiences and student teaching. For secondary preservice teachers, generally, he advocates: educational psychology; philosophy, history, or sociology of education; and practice teaching and special methods.

According to Conant, "the one indisputably essential element in professional education is student teaching" (p. 142). All the rest, he says, should be determined by the entire college or university faculty.

Overall, Conant's position includes a strong general education component, a guarantee that teachers would thoroughly know the subjects they are to teach, and vastly improved student teaching. With regard to pedagogy he is ambivalent, at one time denying its value and at another providing suggestions for its improvement.

2. The TEAM Project: A Preservice Curriculum Drawing Ideas from Researchers and Theoreticians

In 1964, and later in 1967, the American Association of Colleges for Teacher Education (AACTE) published two related documents with implications for the preservice teacher education curriculum. Both resulted from a 27-month, federally sponsored effort titled "A Project to Improve the Professional Sequence in Preservice Teacher Education Through the Selective and Planned Use of New Media." The project became better known as the TEAM Project (Teacher Education and Media).

The first document, referred to as the LaGrone report (1964), was an effort by the project director Herbert LaGrone to present an outline for preservice professional content. After analyzing the factors related to learning, structure, and media, LaGrone suggested five preservice courses with content of common value to all teachers be offered:

1. *Analytic Study of Teaching* giving attention to developing a concept of teaching, based on Smith and Ennis (1961); knowing and being able to use paradigms, models, or schema of teaching, based on Gage (1963) and Maccia et al. (1963); knowing and being able to use four methods to analyze verbal content within the classroom, based on Amidon and Flanders (1963), Bellack and Davity (1963), Smith and Meux (1962), and Taba et al. (1964); knowing

and being able to analyze nonverbal communication in the classroom, based on Hall (1959) and Galloway (1962); assessing the social-emotional climate in the classroom, based on Withall (1949); studying the classroom group as a social system, based on Getzels and Thelen (1960); and gaining knowledge of the nature of leadership style, based on Jenkins (1960).

2. *Structure and Uses of Knowledge* giving attention to typical uses of knowledge, based on Broudy et al. (1964); selecting and using content, based on Hickey and Newton (1964); and understanding how content can be learned and taught, based on Bruner (1962), and so forth.

3. *Concepts of Human Development and Learning* giving attention to the notion of structure of intellect, based on Guilford et al. (1961); cognitive growth, based on Bruner (1964); concept formation, based on Woodruff (1964, *a* and *b*); cognitive learning styles, based on Taba et al. (1964); inquiry training, based on Suchman (1964); readiness and motivation, based on a number of scholars; and evaluation of learning.

4. *Designs for Teaching-Learning*, a course intending to integrate and apply the information obtained in the first three courses, giving attention to teaching strategies, based on Taba et al. (1964) and Smith and Meux (1962); learning unit design, based on Woodruff (1964, *a* and *b*); formation of teaching objectives, based on Bloom et al. (1956) and Mager (1962); instructional systems, based on Lumsdaine (1964); and programmed instruction, based on many sources.

5. *Demonstration and Evaluation of Teaching Competencies* giving attention to teacher behaviors related to teaching and learning; selecting and planning trial experiences followed by teaching and classroom problem solving wherein the above teacher behaviors can be practiced and demonstrated; theories of instruction and teaching, based on Maccia et al. (1963); and analysis of educational issues.

The second document published three years later by the TEAM Project, *Conceptual Models in Teacher Education* (Verduin 1967), contains presentations by leading education researchers and theoreticians, whose work influenced the first TEAM document. This second document elaborates on the suggestions for the five courses advocated by the first document.

Overall, the TEAM project gathered together some of the best thinking available at the time that had possible consequences for preservice teacher education. Somewhat technical in nature it was perhaps too difficult for many practitioners to understand.

3. Teacher Corps: A Teacher Curriculum Fostered by a Politically Sensitive Federal Government

The Teacher Corps was funded under Title V of the Higher Education Act of 1965 (P.L. 89-329) primarily to improve the quality of teachers for schools in low-income urban and rural areas. President Lyndon Johnson, on a surprise visit to the National Education Association's annual convention in

Atlantic City on 2 July 1965, announced its inception, noting that the Teacher Corps would:

> enlist thousands of dedicated teachers to work alongside of local teachers in the city slums and in areas of local poverty. . . . They will be young people, preparing for teaching careers. They will be experienced teachers, willing to give a year to the places in their country that need them the most. (National Advisory Council 1975, p. 1)

Since Teacher Corps was an instrument of federal policy, it was politically sensitive and subject to considerable swings in its recruitment policies and programs.

> The first projects for preservice teachers . . . consisted of about eight weeks of training on teaching disadvantaged children . . . followed by an internship consisting of aiding a teacher (60 percent of the intern's time); taking college coursework (20 percent of the time); the remainder of the intern's time was . . . spent on community projects. (National Advisory Council 1985, p. 5)

However, with the surplus of teachers in the early Seventies, Teacher Corps shifted its training emphasis from "young people preparing for teaching careers" to staff development or retraining and further education of practicing teachers.

Over the years, Teacher Corps has advocated a number of changes in preservice teacher education. Many of these newer emphases were developed under other federally sponsored teacher education projects, but they were mandated to be implemented by funded Teacher Corps projects. They included teaching the disadvantaged (both low-income and learning disabled), recruitment of minority persons, competency-based teacher education, parental involvement, multicultural education, field-based teacher education, and the use of "portal schools" where teachers could be gradually inducted into classrooms.

As a consequence of Teacher Corps training, Teacher Corps graduates were judged to be more effective with their pupils.

> they were found to be superior in . . . developing ethnically relevant curricula, using community resources in teaching and initiating contact with parents, bringing about changes in a child's self-concept. (National Advisory Council 1975, p. 15)

4. CETEM: A Federally Sponsored Effort to Improve Elementary Teacher Education

In 1968 the U.S. Office of Education embarked on a major project with several universities and regional education laboratories to improve preservice elementary education. This project was known as the Comprehensive Elementary Teacher Education Model (CETEM).

As a result of a national competition, federal monies were awarded to Syracuse University, University of Pittsburgh, Florida State University, University of Georgia, Northwest Regional Educational Laboratory, Teachers College Columbia University, University of Massachusetts, the Ohio consortium through the University of Toledo, and Michigan State University. To be a bidder in the competition, applicants had to indicate that their plan for preservice elementary teacher education would meet the following requirements, among others:

1. The goals or outcomes must be stated in terms of teacher competencies (a portent of competency-based teacher education).
2. Selection criteria for entry into the preservice program must be explicit.
3. The professional education curriculum must be explicitly stated in terms of the teacher competencies.
4. The relationship between the professional education curriculum and the rest of the undergraduate program and the graduates' inservice program must be described.
5. Provisions must be made for follow-up studies of graduates.

An analysis of the professional education curriculum in the nine CETEM programs (Cruickshank 1970) found them to contain the following components:

1. Early awareness and engagement, intended to help prospective teachers decide whether a career in teaching was for them
2. Study of classroom communication using observational systems
3. Study of and practice in the technical skills of teaching using microteaching
4. Study of teaching situations using simulation
5. Study of self and interpersonal relations using sensitivity training
6. Child development
7. Human learning
8. Study of how knowledge is produced
9. Study of how to build a curriculum
10. Diagnosis of learning difficulties
11. Problem solving and decision making using simulation
12. School social and cultural dynamics
13. Evaluation
14. Educational technology
15. Role theory
16. Methods of teaching

A second phase of the CETEM competition resulted in 34 bidders submitting proposals to USOE, which required them:

to describe . . . a model teacher training program based upon the specifications designed by one or more of the groups engaged in Phase 1. The remainder of the design becomes the design for a feasibility study of developing, implementing and operation. (from the Request for Proposals)

Unfortunately, because of an oversupply of elementary teachers in the 1970s, the federal government did not provide funds to implement any of the CETEM programs. Still, the activities of CETEM phases one and two generated by aggressive teacher education institutions did result in some new formulations for the preservice curriculum.

5. Teachers for the Real World

In 1966 the U.S. Office of Education, under the National Defense Education Act (NDEA) Title XI, created the National Institute for Advanced Study in Teaching Disadvantaged Youth. The institute's steering committee soon turned its attention from its stated purpose of preparing teachers to serve disadvantaged youth to one of preparing teachers in general. A compilation of the committee's thinking and recommendations was published under the title *Teachers for the Real World* (Smith, Cohen, and Pearl 1969).

In *Teachers for the Real World*, the committee advocated, in keeping with federal policy at that time, the need to prepare teachers with a multicultural point of view. Relatedly, it asked for more preservice teacher experience with disadvantaged youth. Furthermore, the committee advocated provision of appropriate theoretical knowledge to help teachers analyze and understand such new situations as life in inner-city classrooms; provision for training in selected technical skills such as motivating, questioning, and reinforcing; provisions for involvement in the school community; provision of counseling services for preservice teachers; utilization of protocol materials; and creation and utilization of "teacher training complexes."

The committee's proposed program for preservice teacher education has three components: theoretical, training, and teaching field.

The theoretical component, which occurs on campus, would help preservice teachers to interpret and understand what is likely to happen in their classrooms. Thus if conflict is an expected classroom occurrence, then teachers would learn to identify it, understand its origin and nature, and thus be in a better position to resolve it. To provide such preservice education requires a series of curriculum development activities. First, classroom events of educational significance must be identified. These might include classroom transitions, alienated children, cheating, off-task behavior, or conflict. Second, original records or protocols of the events must be prepared. They could be written, or video or audiotaped. Third, the theoretical knowledge that preservice teachers need to know in order to analyze and understand the events depicted in each protocol must be accumulated, for example, the available knowledge about cheating behavior. Finally, preservice teachers are presented with the protocol and the theoretical knowledge that will illuminate it.

Within the theoretical component, preservice teachers would be given numerous protocols of educationally significant events, become aware of theory that illuminates the events, and improve their ability subsequently to interpret and perhaps resolve similar situations. Since not all theoretical knowledge may be learned by analyzing protocols of classroom and school life, there also would be courses wherein additional concepts from the social and behavioral sciences could be learned systematically.

The second component, training, would occur in a public school. Preservice teachers would learn and practice technical skills of teaching with live pupils. Skills might include diagnosing pupil needs, working with different size learning groups, using audiovisual and other technological equipment, and evaluating pupil learning. Additionally, they would be helped with personal professional problems and sensitized to their own feelings, attitudes, and prejudices. Novice teachers would begin working with small groups and gradually take over the entire class.

The teaching field, or subject matter preparation, is the third component. Included in this component are the teachers' subject matter content courses, general education, and "knowledge about knowledge." Suggestions are made for improving both the content and instruction in this component.

Additional elements of the committee's proposed program are the recognition that preservice teachers must be allowed to develop a personally comfortable teaching style and to use that style to its best advantage, and that preservice teachers should develop an understanding of the principles, policies, and procedures of their organized profession.

A paid internship completes the curriculum.

6. An Investigative Reporter's Views on the Teacher Preparation Curriculum

Charles Silberman was commissioned by the Carnegie Corporation Commission on the Education of Educators to undertake a three-year study of the role of the university in educating educators. His report, *Crisis in the Classroom* (1970), actually concentrates on problems that beset American education generally, but three of his chapters do deal specifically with teacher education.

Among Silberman's exhortations with implications for the teacher preparation curriculum are the following:

> The central task of teacher education . . . is to provide teachers with a sense of purpose, . . . with a philosophy of education. This means developing teachers' ability and desire to think seriously, deeply and continuously about the purposes and consequences of what they do. (p. 472)

> They need knowledge about knowledge, about the ramifications of the

subject or subjects they teach, about how those subjects relate to other subjects and to knowledge — and life — in general. (p. 489)

Silberman argues that teachers must become students of teaching more than being merely skillful at teaching a discipline. Unless a teacher is also a student of teaching, "he cannot grow as a teacher" (p. 472). Teachers need insights into their purposes as teachers and how these purposes relate to the school as a social setting, to the values of the local community, and to society in general. Teachers must understand human growth and development, and the nature of mind and thought. Teachers must gain mastery of subject matter in order to provide "a solid foundation and the knowledge of how to learn whatever else he needs to know as he goes along" (p. 491).

Silberman also makes a case for the foundation areas in education. Teachers need to study history and philosophy of education because "they raise continually the sorts of questions that concern the larger goals, setting, and meaning of educational practice" (p. 492, quoting Scheffler 1968). And "the study of psychology, sociology and anthropology also deserve a central place in teacher education" (p. 493), as do the psychology of learning and cognition, dynamics of group behavior, and the sociology and anthropology of the school and community.

With regard to helping teachers understand themselves, Silberman notes:

a growing number of educationists . . . are turning to "sensitivity training" as a means of giving . . . teachers a greater awareness of themselves and of others. (p. 499)

He devotes a full chapter of his book to the liberal education of teachers — one that equips teachers to ask why, and to think seriously and deeply about what they are doing.

Crisis in the Classroom, like Conant's *The Education of American Teachers*, was a best seller and brought the issues and problems of the teacher education curriculum to the attention of the general public.

7. Impact of Research on Teaching on the Teacher Education Curriculum

During the 1970s there was a renewed interest among researchers in studying life in classrooms in order to understand what constitutes teacher effectiveness. Such knowledge could be used to develop a curriculum for a performance-based education of teachers. The movement gained momentum following the release of a study by Rosenshine (1971) and a related writing by Rosenshine and Furst (1971). These two sources contain reviews of 50 studies of teaching that attempt to identify relationships between "process variables," that is, teacher classroom behaviors, and a "product variable," that is, student achievement. Rosenshine's controversial analysis (see Heath and Nielson 1972) suggests five process variables (clarity, variability, enthusiasm, task-oriented or businesslike behavior, and student opportunity to learn criterion material) and has good research support and promise for further study.

Dunkin and Biddle, in their milestone book *A Study of Teaching* (1974), review clusters of studies that focus on a common dimension of teacher behavior such as "teacher talk" or on some classroom phenomenon such as "classroom management and control." The authors present related findings with implications both for teachers and for researchers. Overall, they caution:

> Most findings . . . must presently be presumed tentative because we are not sure how strong they are, because we do not know whether they are independent of other effects, or because they have not yet been validated experimentally. . . . This does not mean that findings in this field are invalid. On the contrary, we suspect that the majority will be confirmed in subsequent research. (pp. 359, 361)

A third review of research on teacher effectiveness was done by Cruickshank (1976). He reports that although some effective teacher behaviors are alike across content and grade levels, others seem to be different. For example, a highly effective pattern for teaching second-grade reading includes: 1) use of small-group instruction, 2) use of a variety of instructional materials, 3) constant teacher monitoring and provision of corrective feedback, and 4) ability of the teacher to maximize direct instructional time in a reading group while maintaining a high level of interaction with students not in the group. On the other hand, effective teachers of fifth-grade reading 1) spend considerable time discussing, explaining, questioning, and generally stimulating cognitive processes; 2) provide considerable independent work; and 3) use a variety of instructional techniques.

Generally, the federally sponsored research reviewed by Cruickshank prompts him to believe that the teacher education curriculum must be specialized, at least in part, in order to prepare teachers to be effective at a particular grade level and with the particular discipline of instruction. This finding provides support that special methods classes indeed are necessary, but that much more attention should be given to the nature of their content.

Soar and Soar (1976) review four of their studies in an effort to identify consistent findings useful to teacher educators. In three of the studies, there is evidence of a relationship between classroom emotional climate and student achievement (negative affect was related to negative gain). A second finding is that closely structured learning activities (greater teacher directness) are related to low cognitive level learning outcomes, while teacher indirectness was related to growth in higher level cognitive activities, for example, creativity. Thus, the Soars conclude that a simple case cannot be made for getting teachers to teach either directly or indirectly. A third finding relates somewhat to the second in that more learning occurs when an intermediate amount of teacher directness is present. Too little or too much is not promising. Consequently, when teacher behaviors are identified that are related to student gain, we need to know what constitutes an optimum amount of that behavior. A fourth related finding supports the idea that greater amounts of pupil freedom are functional for abstract learning tasks. The implication may be that different kinds of achievement outcomes require very different teaching styles (see Powell 1978). One final finding is that the pupil characteristic that most often makes a difference in the way teacher behavior is related to achievement gain is the pupil's socioeconomic status.

Soar's major conclusion is that it is important for teachers to recognize differences in the cognitive level of a learning objective being sought and to provide teacher directness or indirectness, whichever the objective calls for, in the optimum amount.

Medley (1977) presents 613 findings from 14 studies that met stringent criteria for inclusion in his review of research. Generally, he reports that a competent teacher of subject matter is likely to be developing positive attitudes about school as well and that teachers who produce maximum achievement gains are also likely to improve student self-concept the most. He found that there is relatively little difference in the behavior of effective teachers of reading and arithmetic in grade three or below and that patterns of teachers effective with low socioeconomic pupils may differ considerably from those of teachers effective with high socioeconomic pupils. Medley stresses the importance of how teachers use pupil time. He notes that in the ineffective teacher's class the time spent on academic activities is lowest, that there is the most independent and small-group activity, and that the class spends the least time organized into one large group.

Rosenshine and Berliner's review of research (1978) led them to believe that a powerful variable that affects student learning is "academic engaged time," the time that a student spends on academically relevant material of a moderate level of difficulty. Relatedly, they believe that teacher use of "direct instruction" increases academic engaged time. Direct instruction operationally is defined as making goals clear to pupils, allotting sufficient and continuous time for instruction, monitoring pupil progress, asking lower level questions, asking questions that produce mostly correct responses, providing immediate feedback, controlling the instructional goals, and teachers choosing the learning materials and pacing the lessons.

Powell (1978) reviews several studies and concludes that the effective behaviors of teachers vary depending on what is to be learned. For example, the teaching behaviors related to mastery of reading and arithmetic are different from behaviors related to teaching problem-solving skills or guiding independent student work. Relatedly, teacher behaviors related to achievement in grade two and grade five differ for reading and arithmetic. Also, the context of the teaching setting is an important factor. For example, the socioeconomic status of the school community seems to require different teacher behaviors. In addition to her admonition about the need for "different strokes for different folks," she notes, as did Rosenshine and Berliner, that a cluster of direct teacher behaviors — direct instruction — works best when teaching the basic skills of reading and arithmetic in the elementary grades.

The implication for the teacher education curriculum is that since no one pattern or cluster of behaviors will be effective in all instances (all subjects, all grade levels, all pupils), teachers need to learn to use a variety of patterns or clusters of behavior; but all teachers need to be masters of direct instruction for teaching basic cognitive skills.

Good (1983), at the outset of his review, warns that:

> the application of research findings calls for decision making and a careful analysis of teacher context and instructional goals; not blind application. (p. 7)

Then he examines and discusses four promising research areas that have implications for the teacher preparation curriculum: time utilization, classroom management, teacher expectations, and teacher effectiveness research generally.

Regarding time usage, Good notes that measures of academic learning time consistently relate positively to pupil achievement, but that the relationship "is not always substantial." However, this relationship may merely suggest that:

> the teacher possesses minimal managerial skills, the teacher has negotiated some compliance with students, there is an apparent agreed upon direction and purpose in the class, and at least *some* of the time students reflect upon assigned work. (p. 13)

What researchers and teacher educators must address besides the *quantity* of engaged learning time is the *quality* of the time expenditure. For example, what kinds of instruction get diverse students interested in diverse learning tasks.

Regarding classroom management, Good, as does Dunkin and Biddle (1974), sees much to recommend in the work of Kounin (1970), who found that good classroom managers use techniques that prevent misbehavior. These techniques include with-it-ness, momentum, alerting, and overlapping. Good also notes a study by Emmer et al. (1980), which found that effective classroom managers of grade three were superior because their rules, procedures, and expectations of pupil conduct were clear, and there was a commitment to teach the management system to pupils. Relatedly, Good reports that Evertson and Anderson (1979) found that better managers carefully monitored pupil behavior and dealt with misbehavior more quickly.

Regarding teacher expectations, Good points out that teachers should know that they frequently differentiate their behavior toward pupils perceived as high or low achievers, that their expectations are communicated in a variety of ways, that they can expect too much or too little, and that they sometimes treat pupils too much alike.

Regarding teacher effectiveness, Good notes that in his studies of teaching arithmetic in fourth grade and in the junior high school he found "active teaching" was important. Active teaching requires teachers to be more active in presenting and explaining the meanings of concepts, to provide appropriate practice, and to monitor practice prior to assigning seatwork. Active teachers seek to confirm that students understand, a finding reported also by researchers on teacher clarity (Cruickshank, Kennedy, Bush, and Myers 1979; Hines 1981).

Other teacher effectiveness literature that has implications for the teacher preparation curriculum includes: Borich (1979), Brophy (1979), Doyle (1979, 1983), Gage (1978), Griffin (1983), and Stallings (1982, 1983).

8. Teacher Education in Ohio: A State Takes Its Pulse

In 1972 the Commission on Public School Personnel Policies in Ohio distributed *Realities and Revolution in Teacher Education*, in which the deficiencies of teacher education in that Midwestern state were enumerated and the impediments to progress cited. According to the report, the curriculum in teacher education was not working because: 1) what was taught had little transfer to the realities of classroom practice, 2) much of what was taught could be better learned in schools, 3) too much was expected in too little time, and 4) Ohio teacher education institutions taught about teaching but gave little opportunity to practice what was learned.

Calling for widespread changes, including a five-year preparation program, the commission recommended the new curriculum attend to giving preservice teachers: 1) command of theoretical knowledge about learning and human behavior, 2) control of technical skills that appear to facilitate student learning, 3) control over the subject matter to be taught, and 4) help in developing attitudes that foster learning and genuine human relationships. The commission also advocated a carefully sequenced program of professional on-campus and field-based clinical and laboratory experiences. The learning experiences would include focused observation, teacher aide experience, tutoring, simulations, microteaching, student teaching, and community projects. Overall, the report presents a rich array of ideas, some old and some new, for curriculum improvement.

9. Teacher Education for Community Building: Power to the People

The Study Commission on Undergraduate Education and the Education of Teachers was established by the U.S. Office of Education in 1972 to be a voice for the poor, powerless, and oppressed. The Study Commission, which functioned from 1972 to 1976, was made up of more than 50 persons representing stakeholders in undergraduate teacher education. Its major publications were *Teacher Education in the United States: The Responsibility Gap* (1976), *The University Can't Train Teachers* (Olson, Freeman, Bowman, and Pieper

1972), and *Education for 1984 and After* (Olson, Freeman, and Bowman 1972).

Among the major general premises guiding the work of the Study Commission were that: 1) local control of education and teacher education is highly desirable, even necessary, 2) teacher training should mostly take place in the field in community-controlled schools, 3) education and teacher education must recognize and support cultural pluralism (see section on Multicultural Teacher Education), and 4) teacher training should use a diversity of curricula and methods.

Among the suggestions and recommendations related to the preservice curriculum in the final report, *The Responsibility Gap*, are that: 1) preservice teachers should have experiences in local communities; 2) the teacher education curriculum should concentrate more on skills and competencies, sympathy for and understanding of children, and ability to work successfully with others; 3) programs should produce teachers who can work effectively in both classroom *and* community; 4) the curriculum must prepare teachers for community helping and community building; and 5) the curriculum should offer the preservice teachers "a perspective which might encourage them to change something" and insights "needed to make education serve the interests and survival needs of a child's class, culture and person."

The Study Commission's strong commitment to the concept of school-based teacher education is epitomized in the following statement from *The University Can't Train Teachers:*

> The professional aspect of the training of teachers needs to be centered in the schools and controlled by them as a "technical training" comparable in some ways to industrial training. The role of higher education in the education of teachers may be to provide a good general or liberal education in the first three years of college. School-based professional training should be offered in the fourth and possibly fifth years. . . . School-based professional training should include a strong component of teaching by the community, and control by parents and students. It should respect the life-style, value system, language and expressive system of the culture in which the school which provides training is located: both teacher trainees and the IHE training faculty should respond to these culture aspects. (p. vi)

The work of the Study Commission reflects the social unrest in America in the 1960s and 1970s. Such concerns were recognized by persons in teacher education, but whether this recognition was sufficient is another matter. With the shortfall in federal and state funds to support teacher education, the concept of "teacher as community builder" seems to have been displaced by more recent economic and political challenges.

10. Promoting Cultural Pluralism: Multicultural Teacher Education

The 1960s and 1970s in America was a period of social and political ferment. This was the time of "movements" to elevate the status of blacks, Chicanos, native Americans, women, homosexuals, and the handicapped. The mood of the times was that everyone matters, everyone counts! Among these various movements was one aimed primarily at the education establishment; this was multicultural education, which was intended to enhance the self-concepts of all minority children in America's classrooms by establishing that their cultures are worthy and, in fact, exemplary. It also intended to inform majority children that minorities had made significant contributions to American life.

> Multicultural education recognizes cultural diversity as a fact of life in American Society, and it affirms that this cultural diversity is a valuable resource that should be preserved and extended. ("No One Model American" 1973, p. 264)

The long-range outcome would be the positive transformation of adult attitudes toward minorities by members of the dominant culture. Thus, the immediate task for teachers was to teach *all* children to know and respect *all* Americans. The impact of the movement on public school education was broad. Among other things, schools were urged to:

1. Examine texts for evidence of racism, classism, and sexism.
2. Develop new curricula providing opportunities to learn about and interact with a variety of cultural groups.
3. Organize the curriculum around universal human concerns that bring cultural perspectives to bear on issues.
4. Create school environments that radiate cultural diversity.
5. Recognize, accept, and use bilingualism as a positive contribution.

The multicultural movement has also had a considerable impact on teacher education. For example, the most recent NCATE *Standards* (1982) require that:

> The institution provides for multicultural education in its teacher education curricula, including both the general and professional studies components. (p. 14)

NCATE suggests that the multicultural education of teachers include experiences for preservice teachers that:

> (1) promote analytical and evaluative abilities to confront issues such as participatory democracy, racism and sexism and parity of power; (2) develop skills for values clarification including the study of the manifest and latent transmissions of values; (3) examine the dynamics of diverse cultures and the implications for developing teaching strategies; and (4) examine linguistic variations and diverse learning styles as a basis for the development of appropriate teaching strategies. (p. 14)

57

In addition, the Philosophy of Education Society has also supported "selected and appropriate elements related to multicultural education . . . in teacher education programs" (Philosophy of Education Society 1980).

Other contributions to the multicultural teacher education movement include: publication by the AACTE Commission on Multicultural Education and the Committee on Performance-Based Teacher Education of the book, *Multicultural Education Through Competency-Based Education* (Hunter 1974); establishment of the AACTE Ethnic Heritage Center for Teacher Education with support from Title IX of the Elementary and Secondary Education Act; and revision of various states' teacher education standards. For example, Ohio now calls for the teacher education curriculum to give attention to:

> human relationships related to both teaching in a culturally pluralistic society and working with students regardless of race, political affiliation, religion, age, sex, socioeconomic status or exceptionality. (Ohio Department of Education 1975, p. 4)

The Teacher Corps and the Higher Education Act of 1965 have also promoted acceptance of cultural diversity.

Arciniega (1977) has offered teacher educators a profile of an ideal teacher of multicultural education. Among other things, he calls for preparing teachers who believe cultural diversity is worthy, who have a commitment to enhancing the minority child's self-image, who have confidence in culturally different children's ability to learn, who possess knowledge of culturally and linguistically different children, who have literacy in a minority language or dialect, who have skill in successful approaches to teaching culturally different students, and who are willing to participate in minority community activities.

Many colleges and universities report that they now include multicultural education in the preservice curriculum (Commission on Multicultural Education 1978). On the other hand, Banks (1977) has noted:

> There has been little calm and serious public debate concerning multi-ethnic education among educators. Why? There is certainly no lack of divergent beliefs. . . . The answer lies . . . in the explosiveness of the topic. The ethnic studies movement was born in the midst of a highly politicized and radically tense period. Scholars and educators have allowed strong emotions to overwhelm them in discussions of ethnicity and schooling. (p. 695)

11. Teaching as Helping Through Artistry

> The good teacher is not one who behaves in a given way. He is an artist, skillful in facilitating effective growth in students. To accomplish this he must use methods appropriate to the complex circumstances he is involved in. His methods must fit the goals he seeks, the children he is working with, the philosophy he is guided by. (Combs et al. 1974, p. 7)

58

In the Sixties and Seventies, Arthur Combs and others at the universities of Florida, Northern Colorado, and Massachusetts advocated a highly personal, idiosyncratic view of teaching. They shunned the view that good teachers are somehow alike, contrary to what researchers on teaching have attempted to prove.

> The good teacher is no carbon copy but possesses something intensely and personally his own. Artists sometimes call this "the discovery of one's personal idiom." The good teacher has found ways of using himself, his talents, and his surroundings in a fashion that aids both his students and himself to achieve satisfaction. (Combs et al., p. 8)

Thus Combs defines the effective teacher:

> as a unique human being who has learned to use himself effectively and efficiently to carry out his own and society's purposes in the education of others. (Combs et al., p. 8)

For Combs and his associates the task of the teacher education curriculum is to assist the preservice teacher in "becoming," that is, learning how to use one's "self-as-instrument."

Advocates of the self-as-instrument point of view eschew stimulus-response psychology and psychoanalytic theories because they lead to mechanistic and atomistic ways of working with persons. Rather, they embrace what is called a "Third Force" psychology, which regards humans, not as things to be manipulated and molded, but as organisms in the process of self-development and becoming. Third Force psychologists, more specifically perceptual psychologists, argue that behavior is a function of perception, that is, how one sees oneself and sees situations in which he is involved. Third Force psychologists believe that a good teacher education should be concerned primarily with helping preservice teachers to be in touch with themselves — their feelings, attitudes, and beliefs about subject matter, people, and purposes of learning. It would:

> help each student find the methods best suited to him, to his purposes, his task, and the peculiar populations and problems with which he must deal on the job. (Combs et al., p. 26)

A preservice teacher education curriculum based on the self-as-instrument concept would involve students in continuous exploration of self and others, ideas and purposes, as they relate to problems of the classroom. This on-going exploration would include learning experiences that confront preservice teachers with professional problems and engage them in personal decision making to find solutions (Combs 1978, p. 560). Personal discovery would be enhanced through counseling, group experiences, sensitivity training, and other awareness techniques.

In the 1970s the University of Florida initiated such a preservice teacher education program with Combs as its architect. The program centers on three kinds of experiences: 1) field experiences that provide early and continuous exposure to children and youth in natural classrooms and in the community; 2) substantive panels that offer broad exposure to ideas through individual and group study and interaction with faculty specialists; and 3) the seminar, in which a stable, base group explores the personal meaning of experiences encountered during the process of becoming a teacher.

The University of Florida's field experience program begins with the preservice teacher working with one or a few children for four hours a week and continues for at least four quarters, with increasing responsibility until finally the novice assumes the role of a full-time teacher. Throughout their varied field experiences, preservice teachers are exposed to different types of teaching and classroom organization, interact with varied types of students of different ages, and experience life in the community. The field experiences serve as the vehicle for learning about and confronting real problems, student diversity, and teaching diversity; provide a place where strengths and weaknesses become known; and offer a setting where preservice teachers can try out their capacities to cope.

Substantive panels are intended to expose preservice teachers to professional ideas. A panel, staffed by regular faculty, provides sessions that stimulate the preservice students to think about professional information and technique in their special areas of interest. The panels begin with orientation sessions that explain how students can proceed to study in their area and are followed with optional small group meetings and scheduled individual conferences. Then students, either independently or in small groups, develop work contracts that are negotiated with the faculty.

The seminar serves as the home base for 30 preservice teachers and one faculty member. The primary purpose of the seminars is to create a setting wherein students can discover personal meaning through the ideas and experiences to which they have been recently exposed.

Throughout the Florida program, experiential learning is emphasized. Teacher education faculty are not so much teachers as counselors, skilled in helping each student find out how best to become a unique helper of children and a classroom artist. What distinguishes the preservice teacher education formulated by Combs and his associates is its greater attention to *how* the curriculum should be presented.

12. Performance/Competency-Based Teacher Education

Performance- or competency-based teacher education (CBTE) was a major national effort at curriculum reform, which had its origins in the Comprehensive Elementary Teacher Education Model (CETEM) with support from the Educational Testing Service National Commission on Performance-Based Education (McDonald 1974) and the AACTE Committee on Performance-Based Education (1974). Among other things, this was an effort to base the teacher preparation curriculum on specific teaching competencies.

Several ways of identifying these competencies were proposed: 1) they could be gleaned from research on those teaching abilities that are related to pupil achievement; 2) they could be provided by experienced educators judged to be experts; 3) they could be derived from polls of stakeholders in education; 4) they could be culled from the literature, for example, CETEM programs; 5) they could be extracted from different teacher roles such as those described by Joyce and Weil (1972); and 6) they could result from task analyses of teaching at different levels and in different curriculum areas. All of these approaches have been used, resulting in numerous competency lists, for example, *Florida Catalog of Teacher Competencies* (Dodl et al. 1972) and *Generic Teaching Competencies* (Pennsylvania Department of Education 1973).

Once identified and agreed upon, the competencies are stated in terms of observable teacher behaviors. Then curriculum materials or learning modules are developed. An example of such modules is the National Center for Research in Vocational Education's *Handbook for the Development of Professional Vocational Teacher Education Modules* (1973), which includes performance objectives; references, equipment, and materials needed; alternate learning experiences; and supplements (see Houston 1972). Through the use of such modules, the preservice teacher is expected to be able to perform one or more competencies.

The broad categories of competencies included in the modules cover such areas as: assessing and evaluating student behavior, planning instruction, implementing instruction, performing administrative duties, communicating verbally and nonverbally, developing personal skills, and developing pupil self (Dodl et al. 1972, p. 6).

With its emphasis on identifying and gaining consensus on requisite teacher competencies, the CBTE movement was a major influence on preservice curriculum development and later provided the impetus for the teacher competency testing movement.

13. Personalizing Teacher Education (PTE)

The late Frances Fuller and others at the Research and Development Center for Teacher Education at the University of Texas believed that the traditional preservice curriculum was not in harmony with the psychological needs of preservice students (Fuller and Bown 1975). Her explanation for why preservice students frequently complain that education courses are not relevant is that they probably are not ready to benefit from them. Her research supports that conclusion.

First she conducted a survey of studies dealing with the problems of preservice and beginning teachers. Her conclusions from that survey were that:

> what we know is that beginning teachers are concerned about class control, about their own content adequacy, about the situations in which they

teach and about evaluations by their supervisors, by their pupils. (Fuller 1969, p. 216)

Fuller contended that the survey findings make it clear that preservice students' concerns are not what are commonly included in education courses, such as instructional design, methods of teaching, assessment of learning, child development, and so forth.

Next Fuller set out to identify the concerns of student teachers by involving them in small-group sessions led by counseling psychologists. The sessions were tape recorded. Analysis of the statements made by the student teachers indicated that:

> concern with the parameters of the new school situation and with discipline were . . . the most frequently mentioned topics during the early weeks. Concern with pupils and pupil learning was more frequent during later weeks. . . . On the one hand was concern with self, i.e., concern with self-protection and self-adequacy: with class control, subject matter adequacy, finding a place in the power structure of the school and understanding expectations of supervisors, principal and parents. On the other hand was concern with pupils: with their learning, their progress and with ways in which the teacher could implement this progress. (p. 211)

Fuller followed up her initial research by involving 29 student teachers in informal post-luncheon discussions with a counseling psychologist. Periodically they were asked to respond in writing to the question, "What are you concerned about now?" Fuller's analysis of the responses supported her earlier findings, that is, that student teachers are mostly concerned with selves — "where they stood" and "how adequate they were."

In order to answer the question, "Do self concerns persist?" Fuller reviewed studies of perceived problems of experienced teachers. She again concluded (despite some contradictory evidence) that early concerns seem to be concerns with self, while later concerns seem to be concerns about pupils.

As a result of her research, Fuller formulated a three-phase developmental model of teacher concerns: 1) Pre-teaching phase — non-concern with teaching problems; 2) Early teaching phase — concern with self; 3) Later teaching phase — concerns with pupils.

As a consequence of her work, Fuller and her associates advocated a Personalized Teacher Education program (Fuller 1974), the curriculum for which would be sequential in terms of personal-professional development, that is, starting with concerns about self, then moving on to concerns about the teaching task and concerns about benefits to pupils.

Implementing PTE requires collecting considerable personal information about preservice students, using self-reports, psychological instruments, and self-observations involving videotaping. Once the information is collected, it is presented to the student in such a way that the student can observe discrepancies between self-perceptions, observation of actual behavior, and some standard of performance. The intent always is to use the information to move the student toward the higher phase of teaching concerns, that is, concern for pupils. Thus the ultimate goal of PTE is to give prospective teachers a personalized education themselves, so they in turn can provide one for their pupils.

14. The Teacher as Actor: Teacher Education as Role Acquisition

Robert Travers suggests that it is not enough for preservice students to know what roles and abilities they must acquire in order to become effective classroom performers. They must also learn *how* to acquire those roles and abilities. In his writings (Travers 1975; Travers and Dillon 1975), he turns to the theater and the work of the famous Russian director Stanislavski, the founder of method acting, since he feels that "those who know most about techniques for learning roles are those concerned with teaching in the theatre arts." Stanislavski's work appealed to Travers because it called for the actor to become totally immersed in a role rather than merely saying the correct words and performing required actions. Stanislavski, says Travers, was "appalled by what he saw [among actors] as striving for surface polish and surface technical perfection." Acting must be authentic rather than mechanical. To play the role of Julius Caesar, the actor has to become the living reincarnation of Caesar. He must embrace all of Caesar's feelings and beliefs. Similarly, to be an effective teacher, the preservice student has to become completely immersed in that role.

To immerse preservice students in the role of effective teacher, Travers borrows five procedures from Stanislavski: 1) studying the role, 2) searching for material through which the role can be achieved, 3) searching for role sources within the individual, 4) preparing to enter the classroom, and 5) searching for creative ways to keep the role alive.

Studying the Role. Preservice students first have to understand what roles and abilities they must acquire in order to become effective teachers. Travers is critical of the customary practice of sending students into natural classrooms to observe teachers because the role model they observe may be a negative one, for example, the teacher as an authoritarian. Instead, he proposes using film of effective teachers demonstrating the roles and abilities that contribute to their effectiveness. By viewing and analyzing such films, the preservice student can then speculate as to how effective teachers might both feel and function in a range of classroom situations beyond those illustrated in the film. Thus the preservice student sees the effective teacher in a specific circumstance, analyzes why the performance is effective — cognitively and affectively — and speculates how an effective teacher would behave under numerous other circumstances.

Searching for Material Through Which the Role Can be Achieved. Preservice students must be exposed to exemplars of effective teaching both to study and as a source of ideas. However, they must be warned against attempting to copy the role modeled by a particular teacher. Rather, they must learn how to formulate significant questions about teachers, understand the nature of teaching, know the problems involved, and discover some of the techniques and resources that can be adapted from exemplary teachers to make them their own.

Besides studying models of exemplary teachers, preservice teachers also must learn the subject matter they are to teach and ways that it can be taught. All this must be done in relationship to their personalized, authentic concept of role. Thus their concept of role will determine the way preservice students will teach and, to some extent, the content of instruction.

Searching for Role Sources Within the Individual. An attribute of effective teachers is clarity. Teachers cannot pretend to be clear. If they are not clear, they must learn how to become so, or else choose a profession other than teaching. Once a personal, authentic role of teaching has been identified, then preservice students must find within themselves the aptitudes requisite to assuming the role.

Preparing to Enter the Classroom. Travers believes that preservice students will not profit from working in natural classrooms until they have grasped the basic concepts of role learning, which is not to copy what another does but rather to observe the teaching of pupils in order to add to one's own resources, and to recognize that even exemplary teachers will manifest practices that do not fit one's own role. Travers suggests that the first thing novice teachers must learn to do on entering a classroom is to become comfortable and tension free. When that is achieved, they should have opportunities for nonstressful interactions with the entire class. This gradual induction into the dynamics of a classroom provides time during which novices can practice their roles with increasingly larger numbers of pupils. Travers calls for a "role trainer" to help the novice gain insight into role development and performance. The trainer might be akin to an acting coach.

Searching for Creative Ways to Keep the Role Alive. Travers sees teaching as a developmental process that needs continuing nurturance. Teachers must be ever-ready to modify their role and to search for material and for sources within themselves through which the modified role can be achieved.

15. America's Bicentennial Provides a Flagship Curriculum

The report by AACTE's Bicentennial Commission on Education for the Profession of Teaching, *Educating a Profession* (Howsam et al. 1976), was an effort to stimulate debate and discussion on several aspects of teacher education, including the curriculum. Urging that "the profession must establish consensus on the professional culture required to *begin* the practice of teaching," the report suggests that the major curriculum components should be as follows:

1. General or liberal studies to meet a teacher's professional as well as personal needs. It recommends that:

> all prospective teachers participate in an experience focusing on the
> nature and implications of knowledge in conjunction with general educa-
> tion studies. . . . Students will consider alternative ways of knowing,
> unique structures of knowledge in the different fields, linkages among
> concepts in the various disciplines, and the implications of these ideas for
> teaching at the elementary and secondary level. (p. 82)

2. Pre-education in the undergirding disciplines that provide much of the theoretical base from which educational practice is drawn, for example, psychology, sociology, anthropology, and philosophy.

3. Preparation in an academic specialization requiring study in the area or areas in which one will teach. Such study should be designed to enable prospective teachers "to think analytically, act wisely, and excite others about the value of the discipline."

> Of critical importance to the subject matter preparation of teachers is at-
> tention to the broad principles and generalizations of a subject, rather
> than concentration on a maze of specific topics. (p. 86)

4. Foundations of education as a professional component that provides:

> interdisciplinary and conceptual illumination of the issues, problems and
> procedures confronting contempory educators everywhere so that more
> professional and humane public action might ensue. (p. 87)

Clearly, the intent is to promote professional activism in teachers.

> The student must develop a sense of social purpose — an activistic con-
> cern for the sociopolitical *ends* of the educational experience which invest
> professional discussions and procedures with ultimate meaning and con-
> viction. (p. 87)

5. Professional knowledge base that prepares teachers to analyze and subsequently gain understanding and control of classroom events. The professional knowledge base is gained through the study of theoretical knowledge, that is, linked with the study of actual situations in classrooms and schools.

6. Teaching behaviors and skills to meet a teacher's professional requirements. In addition to a knowledge base enabling teachers to understand and analyze life in classrooms, they also need a broad repertoire of generic classroom skills in diagnosis and evaluation, organizing classrooms, setting goals and objectives, planning, communication, instruction, and interpersonal relations (pp. 160-161).

7. Teacher values and attitudes "to provide preservice teachers with a philosophy of education that will help them to think seriously and continuously about the purposes and consequences of what they do" (p. 89).

8. Professional literacy to provide preservice teachers with opportunities to become knowledgeable about educational and sociopolitical issues and to prepare them to interact with concerned citizens in the resolution of such issues.

9. Field experiences to meet the preservice teacher's need to relate theory and practice.

10. Learning disabled children to provide preservice teachers with preparation to work with mainstreamed children having a variety of learning disabilities.

11. Study of a significant subculture to meet preservice teachers' needs to practice in and adjust their performance to divergent school and community environments.

The AACTE Bicentennial Commission report is probably the most comprehensive set of recommendations for the teacher education curriculum ever written by the teacher education establishment.

16. Raising Teachers' Sights: Helping Teachers Become Better Problem Solvers and Decision Makers

Over the past 15 years, Donald Cruickshank and colleagues at Ohio State University, University of Tennessee, and State University of New York at Brockport have tried to help preservice students develop higher level professional cognitive skills, namely, analysis, synthesis, evaluation, and problem solving. They have developed two kinds of curriculum materials for this purpose. The first uses simulations to help preservice students study and resolve problems of practicing teachers. The second is a method called "Reflective Teaching" that is designed to make preservice students more thoughtful about their teaching. Both of these methods are discussed more fully in Part III.

In order to prepare preservice students for the reality of problems teachers face in the classroom, several field studies were conducted (Cruickshank and Leonard 1967; Cruickshank and Broadbent 1968; Cruickshank, Kennedy, Leonard, and Thurman 1968; Cruickshank, Kennedy, and Myers 1974). K-12 teachers were first asked to provide first-person, diary-like accounts of their classroom concerns and then to respond to checklists containing statements about these concerns that the investigators had extracted from the accounts. Those concerns that were noted by teachers as most frequent and most bothersome became the bases for the development of two simulations (Cruickshank, Broadbent, and Bubb 1967; Cruickshank 1969). In each simulation trainees assume the role of a new teacher. Following an orientation to the school and school district where they would work, trainees are given pupil cumulative record folders and other job-related information. After assimilating such information, trainees are next exposed to a number of the classroom problems on film, in role plays, and in written incidents. The task is to try to resolve each problem in order to reach the desired teacher goal with the fewest negative side effects for others (pupils, parents, administrator, or other teachers).

Also, Cruickshank, Applegate, Holton, Mager, Myers, Novak, and Tracey (1980) have identified and organized the educational theory associated with five prevalent areas of teacher concern: affiliation, control, parent relationships and home conditions, student success, and time management. With the theory as a base, preservice students are then given problem-solving situations that they are to resolve in a straightforward, systematic fashion. This direct engagement with the problems of practice is intended to help preservice students become aware of the more difficult and challenging aspects of classroom life and to help them become better problem solvers.

In *Reflective Teaching* (Cruickshank et al. 1980), the intention is to make preservice students more thoughtful students of teaching. The materials include a number of specially developed brief lessons that preservice teachers use for on-campus peer teaching in cognitive, psychomotor, or affective domains. Several preservice students concurrently teach small groups of peers one of the lessons. After 15 minutes of teaching, the teachers test their learners to determine what learning has occurred. They also assess learner satisfaction. For 20 minutes thereafter, each teacher and the group of peer learners use guided discussion to reflect on the process and results. Finally, the small groups reassemble, and the college instructor continues the discussion focusing on the question: What have we learned about teaching and learning?

The goal of both simulations as described herein and of Reflective Teaching is to prepare teachers for the realities of life in classrooms and to make them aware of why they are doing what they are doing.

17. Preparing Professional Teachers in Schools of Pedagogy

Eleven years after publication of *Teachers for the Real World* (Smith, Cohen, and Pearl 1969), B.O. Smith, in collaboration with colleagues at the University of South Florida, presented a second conceptualization for the preparation of teachers in *A Design for a School of Pedagogy* (Smith, Silverman, Borg, and Fry 1980).

In this publication the main point made is that teacher education has become deprofessionalized. As teacher education moved from normal schools and teachers colleges to university campuses, academic knowledge was emphasized and pedagogy subtly downgraded. According to Smith et al., teachers colleges "came to be nothing more than a liberal arts school with a service department of pedagogy to provide a minimum of professional preparation." *A Design for a School of Pedagogy*, as the title implies, suggests the creation of new schools of pedagogy to correct the inadequacies of current university teacher education.

Among its many proposals, the report recommends that the four-year undergraduate curriculum leading to a bachelor's degree should be followed by two years in a school of pedagogy leading to a master of pedagogy degree. In the bachelor's degree program, the major focus should be on preparing teachers in the subjects they will teach and complementary subjects for both prospective secondary and elementary teachers. Additionally, at this level students should receive a solid background in the social and behavioral sciences underlying pedagogy to ensure a foundation for studying professional education.

In the school of pedagogy, the entire curriculum focus would be on pedagogy, learning the science and art of teaching. Areas covered during the fifth and sixth years in approximate order are: clinical knowledge and skill in observation; exceptionality; pedagogical psychology (observation, diagnosis, planning, management, grouping, instruction, communication, evaluation); measurement and evaluation; school and community; curriculum and instruction; curriculum of the school; content selection and organization; selection of curriculum materials; specialized courses in specific curriculum areas; field experiences in clinical complexes; clinical seminars using protocols; and student evaluation and remediation.

According to the authors, if such six-year preservice programs were established, much could be done to right the conditions that have deprofessionalized teacher preparation. These new programs would be able to draw on the recent research on school and teacher effectiveness. *A Design for a School of Pedagogy* seems to be the basis for statewide renewal of teacher education in Florida (Smith, Silverman, Borg, and Fry 1980).

18. The United Teaching Profession's Plan for the Preservice Curriculum

The teaching profession itself became involved in the preservice curriculum with the publication of the National Education Association's *Excellence in Our Schools: Teacher Education, An Action Plan* (1982). In this document the NEA expressed special concern that

> Teacher education programs must be designed and developed based on what the practitioner says needs to be known and done for beginning effective practice. (p. 7)

Regarding the teacher education curriculum, the report notes:

> All teacher education programs should have three integrated components: liberal arts, at least one subject or teaching specialty, and a professional curriculum. . . . The professional component should focus on classroom practice. Field-based experiences related to all components should be provided throughout the preservice program. (p. 10)

The report goes on to describe three critical functions of teaching that must be the basis for the design, development, and implementation of college programs preparing teachers; presents illustrations of what teachers must know or do in order to perform the above three functions; and provides lists of learnings, skills, and field-based experiences related to the three major functions.

According to NEA, the three major functions of teaching are facilitating learning, managing the classroom, and making professional decisions.

Illustrative of what teachers must know and do related to each function are:

1. To facilitate learning, teachers must know the unique characteristics of students, know student levels of achievement, know student learning problems, identify student interests, work with students individually and in groups, accommodate diversity of learning styles, encourage higher order thinking, and present subject matter.

2. To manage the classroom, teachers must effectively organize the classroom to stimulate learning, communicate with parents and special service personnel regarding students, use community agencies, maintain student records, and facilitate the work of volunteers.

3. To make professional decisions, teachers must decide what to teach, plan priorities, select materials and equipment, and so forth. Professional decision making would occur across, as well as in the context of, the other two major functions.

The above three teaching functions, describing what teachers must know and do, are translated into learnings and skills that suggest the curriculum focus on the following:

1. Human growth and development
2. Knowledge of one or more subjects
3. Knowledge of human behavior
4. Knowledge of learning
5. Knowledge of exceptional children
6. Knowledge of assessment
7. Knowledge of social, cultural, and environmental impacts on learning
8. Knowledge of communication
9. Knowledge of instructional design
10. Knowledge of professional resources (including community agencies) and materials
11. Knowledge of design and evaluation of learning activities
12. Knowledge of legal responsibilities of teachers
13. Knowledge of foundations of public schooling
14. Knowledge of group dynamics
15. Knowledge of the politics of education and related issues
16. Knowledge of the creation and use of student records
17. Knowledge of education research and its interpretation

Additionally, the NEA report recommends a variety of field-based or campus-based laboratory experiences such as:

1. Observation of students, classrooms, teacher conferences, school board meetings, state education department activities, state legislature, professional and learned organizations, and the united teaching profession
2. Microteaching or mirror teaching
3. Conducting case studies of individual students
4. Translating educational theory into classroom practice
5. Participating in curriculum design and development
6. Using instructional technology
7. Classroom teaching

The curriculum proposed by NEA is based on what practitioners say is needed for effective functioning on the first day of school.

19. The Teacher as Molder of the Educated Person: The Paideia Proposal

The Paideia Proposal, An Educational Manifesto (1982) by Mortimer Adler is a plan to reform the K-12 curriculum, but it has clear implications for the preservice preparation of teachers. The plan calls for a single track academic program K-12. Virtually no electives nor vocational preparation is included. The new curriculum would be based on three types of learning that would go on simultaneously in all grades: acquisition of organized knowledge, development of intellectual skills, and enlarged understanding of ideas and values. Adler defined these elements on William Buckley's television program, "Firing Line."

> The first kind of learning is the acquisition of information and organized knowledge and the basic views of subject matter — language, literature, the fine arts, mathematics, natural sciences, history, geography. . . . [This part of the curriculum is aided by teachers] telling, teaching by lecturing, teaching using textbooks and manuals, quizzes, . . . blackboard work. . . . The second kind of learning, in many ways more important, is not the acquisition of knowledge, but the development of intellectual skills in reading, writing, speaking, listening, observing, measuring, estimating, calculating, computing. . . . Coaching is the only way [this part of the curriculum] can be developed. . . . The third kind of learning and teaching is even more important than the second. [It] is the enlargement of the understanding of basic ideas and values [gained by discussion of books] or a work of art. [This type of learning] can't be done by coaching. It can't be done by didactic instruction — by lecturing. It must be done by asking and questioning, the Socratic method . . . people sitting around a table with a moderator. (Buckley 1982, pp. 2-5)

A central premise of Adler's *Paideia Proposal* is that American education is failing, but it can be restored by getting back to the basics. In fact, A. Graham Down, executive director of the Council for Basic Education, notes:

The Paideia Proposal embodies accurately the conception of education the Council for Basic Education has promoted. . . . There are three premises: the principal purpose of schooling is academic, not social; some subjects are more important than others; and all can learn regardless of social or economic background. *(ASCD Update,* March 1983, p. 4)

Turning to preservice teacher education, Adler feels strongly that current teacher candidates are unsuited to learn and current programs in schools of education are unsuited to prepare persons to teach the new curriculum. Says Adler, "I would abolish all schools of education" (Buckley 1982, p. 30). A new generation of teachers would need to be educated in the three primary elements of learning. In the interim, we must select as teachers those who are "on the way" to becoming educated persons. According to Adler, these people will be identifiable because they manifest competence as learners, show strong interest in their personal education, and are motivated to continue learning while teaching.

Addressing the formal teacher education curriculum requisite to producing qualified teachers, Adler notes:

First of all, [they] would have this basic schooling themselves. In the second place, they'd go to four years of college in which . . . there would be a required course of study . . . in which the college courses would be mainly liberal, humanistic in general. . . . Third, I would require of every future teacher that he have three years of clinical practice . . . teaching under supervision — because teaching is an art that requires coaching. (Buckley 1982, p. 30)

All skills of teaching are intellectual skills that can be developed only by coaching, not by lecture courses in pedagogy and teaching methods such as are now taught in most schools or departments of education and are now required for certification. (p. 61)

The publication of *The Paideia Proposal* is significant in that it coincides with the increasing concern for the improved general education of teachers.

20. Readying the Beginning Teacher

Dale Scannell and his colleagues, two of whom had worked on the AACTE bicentennial publication, *Educating a Profession* (Howsam et al. 1976), prepared a follow-up publication, the purpose of which was to define "what teacher characteristics should be guaranteed upon graduation from a teacher education program" and what curriculum would promote development of such characteristics. The publication, *Educating a Profession: Profile of a Beginning Teacher* (Scannell et al. 1983), calls for the preservice curriculum to be organized into four components: general education, preprofessional study in the disciplines undergirding pedagogy, academic specialization, and professional study.

71

Under general education, the proposed curriculum would result in proficiency in the art of communication. Specifically, preservice students would be: 1) proficient in the communication arts (reading, writing, speaking, listening, creative expression, and forms of nonverbal communication); 2) proficient in mathematical skills; 3) proficient in understanding the nature, evolution, and uses of language and how language reflects culture; and 4) proficient in understanding the function, use, and impact of mass communications, the computer, and other technology. Additionally, preservice students would understand groups and institutions, principles of physical and mental health, the relationship between society and work, the relationship of nature and the universe, the relationship of new technologies to human nature, the relationship of time and civilization to values and beliefs, and the fine arts.

Under preprofessional study in the disciplines undergirding pedagogy, the preservice student would "acquire an adequate theoretical foundation in the undergirding disciplines, primarily the social and behavioral sciences such as anthropology, philosophy and sociology." Such study would permit preservice students to understand principles and methods of inquiry related to education and teaching, to understand factors fostering or inhibiting communication, and to know something of the basic disciplines from which teachers draw experience and knowledge.

Under academic specialization, the curriculum would provide preservice students with study of the subjects they eventually will teach. The focus of these studies would be on "the nature of knowledge, the structure of the discipline and the relationship between them, and the processes of inquiry and research."

Under professional studies or pedagogy, the curriculum would consist of four parts: foundational studies in education, generic teaching knowledge and skills, specialized pedagogical knowledge and skills, and field and clinical laboratory experience. Foundational studies include learning and human development, and social, philosophic, historical, and economic policy studies in education. The generic teaching knowledge and skills would help preservice students analyze and interpret student abilities, achievements, needs, and cultural background; design appropriate instruction based on the above analyses; conduct instruction that facilitates learning; manage the classroom; promote effective classroom communication; evaluate learning; and arrange for conferral and referral opportunities. Specialized pedagogical knowledge and skills provide a basis for learning pedagogy related to a specific subject and grade level. Here the curriculum acquaints prospective teachers with what is unique or different about teaching in one situation compared to another. Field and clinical laboratory experience, the final part of professional studies, consists of sequentially planned campus- and field-based experiences, such as simulations, microteaching, Reflective Teaching, observations, and student teaching.

Many of the recommendations in *Profile of a Beginning Teacher* reflect current thought on the teacher education curriculum, similar to those in NCATE's *Standards* (1982), and very similar, as would be expected, to Howsam et al. (1976). However, emphases are on the concept of generic teaching behaviors and on sequentially planned campus- and field-based laboratory experiences.

21. A View from the Captain's Bridge: A Dean Speaks Out

Hendrik Gideonse, dean of the College of Education, University of Cincinnati, suggests that three essential components must provide the underpinnings for the professional education of teachers (Gideonse 1982).

> The first is a sound liberal education and thorough mastery over the content areas to be taught. The second . . . is a thorough exposure to those domains of knowledge and inquiry . . . that inform about the nature of humanity, society and culture. Third, the growing body of professional knowledge . . . must also be mastered. (p. 15)

With regard to liberal education, Gideonse includes literacy, communication and cognitive skills, aesthetics, and values. With regard to the domains of knowledge and inquiry, he recommends study in the humanities and the behavioral and social sciences since, among other things, they:

> define the nature of human development and learning . . . help establish the cultural contexts within which educational goals are defined and served. (pp. 15-16)

With regard to professional knowledge, Gideonse suggests the following curriculum:

1. Instructional alternatives (including use of media)
2. Learner and learning differences
3. Instruction for specific needs of individual learners
4. Curriculum theory
5. Small-group process
6. Professional responsibilities
7. School faculty and staff roles and their interrelationships
8. Parent relationships
9. Classroom management
10. Self awareness

22. A Foundation Makes a Proposal

The Carnegie Foundation for the Advancement of Teaching conducted a three-year study of 16,000 public high schools. Its report, *High School: A Report on Secondary Education in America* (Boyer 1983), deals with the high school curriculum but also calls for improvements in teacher education. The report recommends that:

73

1. Preservice high school teachers should study a common core of subjects paralleling the high school curriculum proposed in the report.

2. Preservice teachers should complete a major in an academic discipline, and significant opportunity for classroom observation should be provided. Prospective teachers should major in an academic subject, not in education.

3. Preservice teachers should have a fifth year of combined instructional and apprenticeship experiences that includes a core of four courses to meet the special needs of teachers. The proposed courses are Schooling in America, Learning Theory and Research, Teaching of Writing, and Use of Technology. The crucial apprenticeship experience would be with a team of master teachers.

Finally, the report calls for a series of one-day Common Learning Seminars to be held during the fifth year, in which preservice teachers would meet outstanding scholar-teachers in the arts and sciences, who would relate the knowledge of their fields to contemporary political and social events.

Summary Recommendations

In the Summary Recommendations in Part I, it was recommended that:

> The numerous teacher education curricula developed over the past century should be identified, organized, analyzed, and presented in such a way that they become a legacy from which to draw.

Part II is an initial effort to do this, in the hope that the results will provide a preliminary, albeit incomplete, repository of ideas gleaned from a selected survey of the teacher education curriculum literature of the past 20 years. This overview of alternative preservice curricula prompts the author to make the following suggestions:

A complete study and report of alternative curricula for teacher education should be undertaken so as to provide an important frame of reference for decision making, and an important historical document;

The philosophic orientations that have guided teacher preparation curricula should be determined more rigorously;

The various proposed curricula content should be organized as a taxonomy to guide the development of future teacher curricula;

New proposed teacher education curricula should be scrutinized and subjected to questions asking so what or what's new;

Teacher educators, as part of their preparation, should be required to be familiar with alternative teacher education curricula and their related issues and problems.

References for Part II

AACTE Committee on Performance-Based Teacher Education. *Achieving the Potential of Performance-Based Teacher Education: Recommendations.* Washington, D.C.: American Association of Colleges for Teacher Education, February 1974.

Adler, M. *The Paideia Proposal: An Educational Manifesto.* New York: Macmillan, 1982.

Amidon, E., and Flanders, N. *The Role of the Teacher in the Classroom: A Manual for Understanding and Improving Teachers' Classroom Behavior.* Minneapolis, Minn.: Paul S. Amidon & Associates, 1963.

Arciniega, T. "Planning and Organizational Issues Involved in Operationalizing the Multicultural Educational Standard." Paper presented at the American Association of Colleges for Teacher Education Leadership Training Institute on Multicultural Education in Washington, D.C., December 1977.

Association for Supervision and Curriculum Development. *Update*, March 1983, p. 4.

Bagenstos, N. "The Teacher as an Inquirer." *Educational Forum* 39 (1975): 231-37.

Banks, J.A. "A Response to Philip Freedman." *Phi Delta Kappan* 58 (May 1977): 695-97.

Barnard, H. *Normal Schools, and Other Institutions, Agencies and Means Designed for the Professional Education of Teachers.* Hartford, Conn.: Case, Tiffany, and Company, 1851.

Bellack, A., and Davity, J. *The Language of the Classroom.* U.S. Department of Health, Education and Welfare Cooperative Research Project No. 1497. New York: Columbia University, Teachers College, Institute of Psychological Research, 1963.

Bloom, B.; Englehart, M.; Furst, E.; Hill, W.; and Krathwohl, D. *Taxonomy of Educational Objectives, The Classification of Educational Goals. Handbook I: Cognitive Domain.* New York: David McKay, 1956.

Borich, G. "Implications for Developing Teacher Competencies from Process-Product Research." *Journal of Teacher Education* 30, no. 1 (1979): 77-86.

Borrowman, M. *The Liberal and Technical in Teacher Education.* New York: Teachers College Bureau of Publications, Columbia University, 1956.

Boyer, E. *High School: A Report on Secondary Education in America.* New York: Harper and Row, 1983.

Brophy, J. "Teacher Behavior and Its Effects." *Journal of Educational Psychology* 71 (1979): 733-50.

Broudy, H. *The Real World of Public Schools.* New York: Harcourt Brace Jovanovich, 1972.

Broudy, H.; Smith, B.; and Burnett, J. *Democracy and Excellence in American Secondary Education.* Chicago: Rand McNally, 1964.

Bruner, J. "The Course of Cognitive Growth." *American Psychologist* 19 (1964): 1-15.

Bruner, J. *The Process of Education.* Cambridge, Mass.: Harvard University Press, 1962.

Buckley, W. F. "The Paideia Proposal." *Firing Line*, public broadcasting network, 7 November 1982.

Combs, A. "Teacher Education: The Person in the Process." *Educational Leadership* 35 (1978): 558-61.

Combs, A.; Blume, R.; Newman, R.; and Wass, H. *The Professional Education of Teachers.* Boston: Allyn and Bacon, 1974.

Commission on Multicultural Education. *Directory: Multicultural Education Programs in Teacher Education Institutions in the United States.* Washington, D.C.: American Association of Colleges for Teacher Education, 1978.

Commission on Public School Personnel Policies in Ohio. *Realities and Revolution in Teacher Education.* Report No. 6. Cleveland, Ohio: Greater Cleveland Associated Foundation, 1972.

Conant, J. *The Education of American Teachers.* New York: McGraw-Hill, 1963.

Corey, S. *Action Research to Improve School Practices.* New York: Teachers College Bureau of Publications, Columbia University, 1953.

Corrigan, D. "American Association of Colleges for Teacher Education, National Education Association Action Plan: Outlines for Reform." *AACTE Briefs* 3, no. 7 (1982): 1-3.

Cruickshank, D.R. "General Education and Teacher Education: What Can We Do to Keep the Texas Rangers Away?" Paper presented at the American Educational Research Association meeting in New York, 1982.

Cruickshank, D.R. "Synthesis of Selected Research on Teacher Effects." *Journal of Teacher Education* 27 (1976): 57-60.

Cruickshank, D.R. *Blueprints for Teacher Education: A Review of Phase II Proposals for the USOE Comprehensive Elementary Teacher Education (CETEM) Program.* Washington, D.C.: U.S. Department of Health, Education and Welfare, 1970. (ERIC Document Reproduction Service No. ED 013 371)

Cruickshank, D.R. *The Inner-City Simulation Laboratory.* Chicago: Science Research Associates, 1969.

Cruickshank, D.R.; Applegate, J.; Holton, J.; Mager, J.; Myers, B.; Novak, C.; and Tracey, K. *Teaching Is Tough.* Englewood Cliffs, N.J.: Prentice-Hall, 1980.

Cruickshank, D.R., and Broadbent, F. *The Simulation and Analysis of Problems of Beginning Teachers.* Research Project No. 5-0789. Washington, D.C.: U.S. Government Printing Office, 1968. (ERIC Document Reproduction Service No. ED 024 637)

Cruickshank, D.R.; Broadbent, F.; and Bubb, R. *The Teaching Problems Laboratory.* Chicago: Science Research Associates, 1967.

Cruickshank, D.R.; Holton, J.; Fay, D.; Williams, J.; Kennedy, J.; Myers, B.; and Hough, B. *Reflective Teaching.* Bloomington, Ind.: Phi Delta Kappa, 1981.

Cruickshank, D.R.; Kennedy J.; Bush, A.; and Myers, B. "Clear Teaching: What Is It?" *British Journal of Teacher Education* 5 (1979): 27-33.

Cruickshank, Donald R.; Kennedy, J.; Leonard, J.; and Thurman, R. *Perceived Problems of Teachers in Schools Serving Rural Disadvantaged Populations: A Comparison with Problems Reported by Inner-City Teachers.* NDEA National Institute for Advanced Study of Disadvantaged Youth Occasional Paper No. 5. Washington, D.C.: American Association of Colleges for Teacher Education, 1968. (ERIC Document Reproduction Service No. 027 986)

Cruickshank, D.R.; Kennedy J.; and Myers, B. "Perceived Problems of Secondary School Teachers." *Journal of Educational Research* 68 (1974): 154-59.

Cruickshank, D.R., and Leonard, J. *The Identification and Analysis of Perceived Problems of Teachers in Inner-City Schools.* NDEA National Institute for Advanced Study in Teaching Disadvantaged Youth Occasional Paper No. 1. Washington, D.C.: American Association of Colleges for Teacher Education, 1967. (ERIC Document Reproduction Service No. 026 335)

Dewey, J. "The Relation of Theory to Practice in Education." In *Teacher Education in America: A Documentary History*, edited by M.L. Borrowman. New York: Teachers College Press, 1965. (originally published in 1904)

Dewey, J. *How We Think*. Chicago: Henry Regnery Co., 1933.

Dodl, N.; Elfner, E.; Becker, J.; Halstead, J.; Jung, H.; Nelson, P.; Purinton, S.; and Wegele, P. *Florida Catalog of Teacher Competencies*. Tallahassee: Florida State University, 1972.

Doyle, W. "Academic Work." *Review of Educational Research* 53 (1983): 159-99.

Doyle, W. "Research on Teaching in Classroom Environments." Paper presented at the National Invitational Conference Exploring Issues in Teacher Education: Questions for Future Research in Austin, Texas, January 1979.

Dunkin, M., and Biddle, B. *A Study of Teaching*. New York: Holt, Rinehart and Winston, 1974.

Elliot, J. "Developing Hypotheses About Classrooms from Teachers' Personal Constructs." *Interchange* 7 (1976-77): 1-22.

Emmer, E.; Evertson, C.; and Anderson, L. "Effective Management at the Beginning of the School Year." *Elementary School Journal* 80 (1980): 219-31.

Evertson, C., and Anderson, L. "Beginning School." *Educational Horizons* 57 (1979): 164-68.

Fuller, F. "A Conceptual Framework for a Personalized Teacher Education Program." *Theory Into Practice* 13 (1974): 112-22.

Fuller, F. "Concerns of Teachers: A Developmental Conceptualization." *American Educational Research Journal* 6 (1969): 207-26.

Fuller, F., and Bown, O. "Becoming a Teacher." In *Teacher Education*, edited by K. Ryan. Chicago: University of Chicago Press, 1975.

Gage, N.L. *The Scientific Basis of the Art of Teaching*. New York: Teachers College Press, 1978.

Gage, N.L. "Paradigms for Research on Teaching." In *Handbook of Research on Teaching*, edited by N.L. Gage. Chicago: Rand McNally, 1963.

Galloway, C. "An Exploratory Study of Observational Procedures for Determining Teacher Non-Verbal Communication." Doctoral dissertation, University of Florida, 1962.

Getzels, J., and Thelen, H. "The Classroom Group as a Unique Social System." In *The Fifty-Sixth Yearbook of the National Society for the Study of Education: Part II*, edited by R. Preston. Chicago: University of Chicago Press, 1957.

Gideonse, H.D. "The Necessary Revolution in Teacher Education." *Phi Delta Kappan* 64 (September 1982): 15-18.

Good, T. "Classroom Research: A Decade of Progress." Paper presented at the meeting of the American Educational Research Association in Montreal, April 1983.

Griffin, G. "Using Research in Preservice Teacher Education." Paper presented for the Improving Preservice Teacher Education Project in Detroit, February 1983.

Guilford, J.; Merrifield, P.; and Cox, A. *Creative Thinking in Children at the Junior High Level*. U.S. Office of Education Cooperative Research Project No. 737. Los Angeles: University of Southern California, 1961.

Gutek, G.L. *An Historical Introduction to American Education*. New York: Thomas Y. Crowell, Harper and Row, 1970.

Hall, E. *The Silent Language*. New York: Doubleday, 1959.

Hall, S. *Lectures to School-Masters on Teaching.* Boston: Carter, Hendee and Company, 1833.

Heath, R., and Nielson, M. "The Research Basis for Performanced-Based Teacher Education." *Review of Educational Research* 44 (1972): 463-84.

Hickey, A., and Newton, J. *The Logical Basis of Teaching: I. The Effect of Subconcept Sequence on Learning.* Newburyport, Mass.: ENTELEK, 1964.

Hines, C. "A Further Investigation of Teacher Clarity: The Observation of Teacher Clarity and the Relationship Between Clarity and Student Achievement and Satisfaction." Doctoral dissertation, Ohio State University, 1981.

Houston, R. *Developing Instructional Modules.* Houston, Texas: University of Houston College of Education, 1972.

Howsam, R.B.; Corrigan, D.; Denemark, G.; and Nash, R. *Educating a Profession.* Washington, D.C.: American Association of Colleges for Teacher Education, 1976.

Hunter, W., ed. *Multicultural Education Through Competency-Based Teacher Education.* Washington, D.C.: American Association of Colleges for Teacher Education, 1974.

Iannone, R. "Current Orientations in Teacher Education." In *Handbook on Contemporary Education,* edited by S. Goodman. New York: Xerox, 1976.

Jenkins, D. "Characteristics and Functions of Leadership in Instructional Groups." In *The Fifty-Ninth Yearbook of the National Society for the Study of Education: Part II,* edited by G. Jenson. Chicago: University of Chicago Press, 1960.

Joyce, B. "The Teacher Innovator: A Program for Preparing Teachers." In *Perspectives for Reform in Teacher Education,* edited by B. Joyce and M. Weil. Englewood Cliffs, N.J.: Prentice-Hall, 1972.

Joyce B. *The Teacher-Innovator: A Program to Prepare Teachers.* Sec. 1 and 2. Washington, D.C.: U.S. Government Printing Office, 1968.

Joyce, B., and Weil, M. *Models of Teaching.* Englewood Cliffs, N.J.: Prentice-Hall, 1972.

Kounin, J. *Discipline and Group Management in Classrooms.* New York: Holt, Rinehart and Winston, 1970.

LaGrone, H. *A Proposal for the Revision of the Pre-service Professional Component of Teacher Education.* Washington, D.C.: American Association of Colleges for Teacher Education, 1964.

Lumsdaine, A. "Educational Technology, Programmed Learning, and Instructional Science." In *The Sixty-Third Yearbook of the National Society for the Study of Education: Part I.* Chicago: University of Chicago Press, 1964.

Maccia, E.; Maccia, G.; and Jewett, R. *Construction of Educational Theory Models.* U.S. Office of Education Cooperative Research Project No. 1932. Columbus: Ohio State University, 1963.

Mager, R. *Preparing Objectives for Programmed Instruction.* San Francisco: Fearon Publishers, 1962.

McDonald, F.J. "The National Commission on Performance-Based Education." *Phi Delta Kappan* 55 (January 1974): 296-98.

Medley, D. *Teacher Competence and Teacher Effectiveness.* Washington, D.C.: American Association of Colleges for Teacher Education, 1977.

Monroe, W.S. *Teaching Learning Theory and Teacher Education.* Urbana: University of Illinois Press, 1952.

National Advisory Council on Education Professions Development. *Teacher Corps: Past or Prologue*. Washington, D.C., 1975.

National Center for Research in Vocational Education. *Handbook for the Development of Professional Vocational Teacher Education Modules*. Columbus: Ohio State University, February 1973.

National Council for Accreditation of Teacher Education. *Standards for the Accreditation of Teacher Education*. Washington, D.C., 1982.

National Education Association. *Excellence in Our Schools: Teacher Education, an Action Plan*. Washington, D.C., 1982.

"No One Model American." *Journal of Teacher Education* 24 (1973): 264-65.

Ohio Department of Education. *Standards for Colleges or Universities Preparing Teachers*. Columbus, 1975.

Olson, P.; Freeman, L.; and Bowman, J., eds. *Education for 1984 and After*. Lincoln: University of Nebraska, 1972.

Olson, P.; Freeman. L.; Bowman, J.; and Pieper, J. *Of Education and Human Community: A Symposium of Leaders in Experimental Education*. Lincoln: University of Nebraska Curriculum Development Center, 1972.

Olson, P.; Freeman, L.; Bowman, J.; and Pieper, J. *The University Can't Train Teachers*. Lincoln: University of Nebraska Curriculum Development Center, 1972.

Pennsylvania Department of Education. *Generic Teaching Competencies*. Harrisburg, June 1973.

Philosophy of Education Society. "Standards for Academic and Professional Instruction in Philosophy of Education." *Educational Theory* 30 (1980): 265-68.

Powell, M. "Research on Teaching." *Educational Forum* 43 (1978): 27-37.

Rosenshine, B. *Teaching Behaviours and Student Achievement*. International Association for the Evaluation of Educational Achievement IEA Studies No. 1. National Foundation for Educational Research in England and Wales, 1971.

Rosenshine, B., and Berliner, D. "Academic Engaged Time." *British Journal of Teacher Education* 4 (1978): 3-16.

Rosenshine, B., and Furst, N. "Research on Teacher Performance Criteria." In *Research in Teacher Education*, edited by B.O. Smith. Englewood Cliffs, N.J.: Prentice-Hall, 1971.

Salzillo, F., and Van Fleet, A. "Student Teaching and Teacher Education: A Sociological Model for Change." *Journal of Teacher Education* 8 (1977): 27-31.

Scannell, D.; Corrigan, D.; Denemark, G.; Dieterle, L.; Egbert, R.; and Nielson, R. *Educating a Profession: Profile of a Beginning Teacher*. Washington, D.C.: American Association of Colleges for Teacher Education, 1983.

Scheffler, I. "University Scholarship and the Education of Teachers." *Teachers College Record* 70 (1968): 1-12.

Silberman, C. E. *Crisis in the Classroom: The Remaking of American Education*. New York: Random House, 1970.

Smith, B.O. *Logical Aspects of Teaching*. Urbana: University of Illinois Press, 1963.

Smith, B.O., and Ennis, H. *Language and Concepts in Education*. Chicago: Rand McNally, 1961.

Smith, B.O., and Meux, M. *A Study of the Logic of Teaching*. U.S. Department of Health, Education and Welfare Cooperative Research Project No. 235. Urbana: University of Illinois, 1962.

Smith, B.O.; Cohen, S.; and Pearl, A. *Teachers for the Real World*. Washington, D.C.: American Association of Colleges for Teacher Education, 1969.

Smith, B.O.; Silverman, S.; Borg, J.; and Fry, B. *A Design for a School of Pedagogy*. Washington, D.C.: U.S. Department of Education, 1980.

Soar, R.S., and Soar, R.M. "An Attempt to Identify Measures of Teacher Effectiveness from Four Studies." *Journal of Teacher Education* 27 (1976): 261-67.

Stallings, J. "Implications from the Research on Teaching for Teacher Preparation." Paper presented for the Improving Preservice Teacher Education Project in Detroit, February 1983.

Stallings, J. "Effective Strategies for Teaching Basic Skills." In *Developing Basic Skills Programs in Secondary Schools*, edited by D.G. Wallace. Alexandria, Va.: Association for Supervision and Curriculum Development, 1982. (ERIC Document Reproduction Service No. ED 216 449)

Stratemeyer, F. "Issues and Problems in Teacher Education." In *Teacher Education for a Free People*, edited by D. Cottrell. Oneonta, N.Y.: American Association of Colleges for Teacher Education, 1956.

Study Commission on Undergraduate Education and the Education of Teachers. *Teacher Education in the United States: The Responsibility Gap*. Lincoln: University of Nebraska Press, 1976.

Suchman, J. *The Elementary School Training Program in Scientific Inquiry*. U.S. Office of Education Title VII Cooperative Research Project No. 216. Champaign-Urbana: University of Illinois, 1964.

Taba, H.; Levine, S.; and Elzey, F. *Thinking in Elementary School Children*. U.S. Office of Education Cooperative Research Project No. 1574. San Francisco: San Francisco State College, 1964.

Travers, R. "Empirically Based Teacher Education." *Educational Forum* 39 (1975): 417-34.

Travers, R., and Dillon, J. *The Making of a Teacher*. New York: Macmillan, 1975.

Verduin, J.R. *Conceptual Models in Teacher Education*. Washington, D.C.: American Association of Colleges for Teacher Education, 1967.

Withall, J. "The Development of a Technique for the Measurement of Social Emotional Climate in Classrooms." *Journal of Experimental Education* 17 (1949): 347.

Woodruff, A. "The Use of Concepts in Teaching." *Journal of Teacher Education* 15 (1964): 81-99.(a)

Woodruff, A. "The Nature and Elements of the Cognitive Approach to Instruction." Mimeographed. University of Utah, 28 May 1964.(b)

Zeichner, K. "Alternative Paradigms of Teacher Education." *Journal of Teacher Education* 34, no. 3 (1983): 3-9.

Part III
Instruction in Teacher Education

The institution shall provide evidence that its faculty uses a variety of instructional procedures which contribute to the students' preparation.
NASDTEC
Standards for State Approval of Teacher Education
1981, p. 10

A friend of mine, a nationally known scholar who teaches in the college of social and behavioral sciences at a major university, recently said to me, "After 30 years I finally know what I want to teach my students; now I must learn *how* I want to teach them." The difference between my friend's admission and similar shortcomings in teacher educators is disturbing. He took no professional education courses to prepare him for teaching. He had no supervised teaching practice.

Why do we so frequently disregard what we know about teaching as we practice teacher education? Why don't we teach as well as we know how to? Are we, as was my friend, so preoccupied with determining the content of instruction that we have no time or interest in determining how that content can best be learned? Not only are we unable to reach consensus on the content of a single professional course, we are also uncertain and inconsistent about how we should teach. We tell preservice students to individualize instruction but seldom do they experience individualized instruction in our classrooms. Or we teach the nature of group process by using the lecture method.

As a modest contribution toward improving the teaching of preservice students, I shall direct my discussion to three questions: What is teaching method? What instructional alternatives are available to teacher educators? What instructional materials are available?

What Is Teaching Method?

Broudy (1963) describes teaching method as:

> the formal structure of the sequence of acts commonly denoted by instruction. The term covers both the strategy and tactics of teaching and involves the choice of what is to be taught at a given time, the means by which it is to be taught, and the order in which it is to be taught. The theories of learning that may or may not have suggested the methods, the aims of the total educative process, and the philosophical considerations that might be used to evaluate them are introduced into the discussion of method, but only as needed to elucidate their nature and import. (p. 3)

A simpler definition of teaching method is, all that teachers think and do from the time they decide to teach something to someone until the time they decide that the teaching is over. Teaching method, then, comprises a whole set of related procedures put into motion by teachers. It includes what they do when preparing to teach, when actually instructing, and when instruction is analyzed and evaluated.

Teaching is highly idiosyncratic. Some teachers are careful planners, while others appear to teach "off the top of their heads." Nevertheless, any consideration of teaching method must address the following questions:

1. What is to be taught? What concepts, skills, and attitudes are to be learned? How can it be determined that they have been learned?

2. What instructional alternatives seem most suitable, given the content and learners at hand?

3. Who or what will provide instruction?

4. How should the learners be organized for instruction (individual, small group, whole class)?

5. Where should instruction take place (field-based or on-campus)?

6. How should the teaching and learning be analyzed and evaluated?

Deciding how instruction will take place requires that the teacher educator be aware of the alternatives available and of their potential for achieving the desired learning outcomes. When teacher educators are unfamiliar with instructional alternatives, they are restricted with regard to overall teaching method.

Following is a selective list of instructional alternatives that could be used by teacher educators.

1. Audiovisuals
2. Centers of interest
3. Debates
4. Deductive discourse
5. Demonstration
6. Discussion (including panels, symposia)
7. Displays and exhibits

8. Experiments
9. Games
10. Inductive discourse
11. Kinesthetic
12. Lecture
13. Microteaching
14. Mirror teaching
15. Observation
16. Programmed instruction
17. Problem solving
18. Protocols
19. Recitation
20. Reflective Teaching
21. Reports
22. Role playing
23. Simulations

In addition to listing instructional alternatives, it is also possible to categorize them along a continuum of experiences from the concrete to the abstract. For example, under concrete experiences we could place kinesthetic methods, microteaching, mirror teaching, problem solving, Reflective Teaching, and simulations. Under vicarious experiences we can place audiovisuals, demonstration, and protocols. And under abstract experiences could go such alternatives as lectures and inductive discourse.

What Promising Instructional Alternatives Are Available For Preservice Teacher Education?

In this section are descriptions and analyses of four instructional approaches to preservice teacher education: microteaching, simulations, Reflective Teaching, and protocols. They have been selected because, in this writer's opinion, they are the most promising alternatives available, even though they are infrequently used. They are promising because they provide for increased amounts of laboratory and clinical practice as called for by the NCATE *Standards* (1982) and other authorities (Howsam et al. 1976; Scannell et al. 1983). They are neglected or used infrequently because they require considerable time to prepare and implement, and because they require teacher educators to assume a role different from that with which they are familiar.

Microteaching

Microteaching is a brief teaching encounter in which preservice students teach five- to twenty-minute lessons in their subject field first to one and then to a small group of pupils, who are usually peers. The purpose of microteaching lessons is to practice a specific technical skill of teaching until the preservice student reaches an acceptable level of performance. Microteaching lessons normally are videotaped.

A microteaching lesson proceeds as follows: First, the student selects or is given a technical skill of teaching to learn and subsequently to practice with a small group of peers on campus. Second, the trainee reads about the skill in one of several pamphlets (Allen et al. 1969). Third, the trainee observes a master teacher perform the skill on film or videotape. Fourth, the trainee prepares a brief lesson to demonstrate the specific skill. The lesson frequently is an abbreviated, partial lesson since time may not permit its completion. Fifth, the lesson is taught to peers and videotaped. (Originally the intent was to teach K-12 students in the schools.) Sixth, the preservice student, college instructor, and peers critique the lesson using the videotape and feedback by peers regarding the teacher's degree of success in demonstrating the skill. Sometimes the lesson may be retaught to a different group of peers to increase the trainee's skill level. If the trainee demonstrates an acceptable skill level, he or she goes on to practice another technical skill. Since teaching technical skills is at the heart of microteaching, it is appropriate to explore these skills in some detail.

Graduate students at Stanford University identified a number of technical skills for the microteaching curriculum at that institution (McKnight 1978). The technical skills included:

1. Establishing set or rapport between pupil and teacher in order to obtain immediate involvement in the lesson;

2. Establishing several appropriate frames of reference through which pupils can gain an understanding of some concept or event;

3. Achieving closure that pulls together the major points learned and acts as a cognitive link between past knowledge and new knowledge;

4. Using effective questions that are appropriate, answerable, and provocative, thus involving pupils actively;

5. Recognizing and obtaining attending behavior and, conversely, recognizing and reducing non-attending behavior;

6. Controlling participation or improving the teacher's ability to analyze and control the use of accepting and rejecting remarks, positive and negative reactions, reward and punishment; and

7. Providing feedback or knowledge of results.

The technical skills were later relabeled and arranged into clusters to show their associations (Allen et al. 1969). The clusters and several skills subsumed under each are reported by McKnight (1978) as follows:

1. Response repertoire. Skills intended to help teachers build verbal and nonverbal techniques in order to help convey meaning, nuance, and mood;

2. Creating student involvement. Skills designed to help teachers stimulate interest and maintain attention, including set induction, stimulus variation, and closure;

3. Questioning skills. Skills designed to give teachers a repertoire of ques-

tioning techniques to stimulate discussion and productive thinking including fluency in asking questions, probing questions, higher-order questions, and divergent thinking questions;

4. Increasing student participation. Skills designed to get students involved including reinforcement, recognizing attending behavior, silence and nonverbal cues, and cueing; and

5. Presentation skills. Skills intended to help teachers present information so that students develop concepts, including completeness of communication, planned repetition, use of examples, and lecturing.

McDonald (1973), one of the originators of microteaching, became critical of the excessive attention given to the original technical teaching skills.

> Unfortunately, the concept of technical skills of teaching has been overly promoted and inaccurately described. They are not basic or essential because there is no data to show that a teacher who uses them produces more effective learning. They may have important effects on learning but that remains to be shown. (p. 55)

Earlier Snow (1969), although less critical, also called for validation of the technical skills.

In the 1970s research by Gage (1976) and Peterson, Marx, and Clark (1978) on set induction, and by Berliner (1976) on probing questions indicated that interest in some of the original technical skills continued. However, work by these and other researchers suggests other skills or reformulations of the original skills indeed may be more promising. For example, accumulating research supports the premise that there are other teaching skills or behaviors strongly and consistently associated with pupil academic gain and satisfaction. Perhaps some of these behaviors, for example, direct instruction, group alerting, clarity, enthusiasm, and high expectations for pupil performance, should be given higher priority than the earlier mentioned technical skills.

Reaction to Microteaching. Whatever its shortcomings, microteaching received a rousing reception from a large segment of the teacher education community. A number of factors account for this. First, it closely followed the acceptance of television as a medium of instruction on university campuses. Second, it was popular among preservice students because they like to see how they are performing on videotape. Third, preservice students have always preferred the direct, firsthand role-taking experiences to abstract ones in their teacher preparation program. Fourth, teacher educators themselves found that microteaching provided a way to give students controlled practice with feedback. Fifth, the innovation was developed by prestigious Stanford University with funding from the Ford Foundation and was disseminated by AACTE under the direction of several well-known educators, including Robert Bush, Dwight Allen, and Frederick McDonald. Finally, the innovation was launched during the Johnson Great Society Years when generous federal funding made possible the installation of new and frequently expensive educational technology.

Research on Microteaching. Copeland (1977) reports that:

> A careful examination of the research pertaining to microteaching indicates . . . that, although laboratory training based on the microteaching model is significantly related to skill exhibition by teacher trainees while teaching in the training laboratory immediately after training, . . . such training has no significant relationship with the tendency of student teachers to exhibit target skills in the classroom weeks after training [in the laboratory] is completed. (p. 148)

Earlier Copeland (1975) had found that students' failure to exhibit the skills learned in a laboratory setting did not seem to be simply a matter of forgetting how to perform the skill once they began their student teaching in a natural classroom. Rather, he determined that the key factor was the influence of the cooperating teachers.

In a series of studies, Copeland found that:

> the cooperating teachers with whom the trainees work in classrooms after completing microteaching training influence the trainee's use of the targeted skills in at least two ways. In the first, labeled "direct influence," cooperating teachers who have been trained in techniques of supervision . . . appear to offer sufficient support and encouragement to assure student teachers' use of target skills in the classroom after training. The second . . . way in which cooperating teachers influence student teaching classroom behavior was labeled by Copeland "indirect influence." His results suggest that student teachers who taught with cooperating teachers who consistently used the targeted skills were significantly more likely to use the skills themselves. (Copeland 1982, p. 1010)

Copeland (1982) also reports other research findings that show that students participating in microteaching evidence increased confidence in themselves and in their teaching abilities and seem to increase in overall levels of self-esteem.

Advantages and Disadvantages. Among the major benefits attributed to microteaching are that:

1. Microteaching is real teaching, involving the student in the direct role of teacher as opposed to role-playing.
2. Microteaching reduces the complexity of the teaching act, allowing concentration on acquiring a specific skill.
3. Microteaching provides an environment in which the focus is on analysis of the teaching act.
4. Microteaching provides a relatively safe and controlled environment in which to practice.
5. Technical skills learned during microteaching can, with the proper reinforcement, result in their use in natural classrooms.

Notable disadvantages seem to include:

1. Microteaching requires considerable time and equipment.
2. Seldom is there time to practice more than a few technical skills.
3. The technical skills currently used may not be as important as others that have been found to be associated with effective teaching.

Materials to Support Microteaching. Following are sources useful to those wishing to utilize microteaching.

Allen, D., and Ryan, K. *Microteaching.* Reading Mass.: Addison-Wesley, 1969.

Allen, D.; Bush, R.; Ryan, K.,; and Cooper, J. *Teaching Skills for Elementary and Secondary Teachers.* New York: General Learning Corporation, 1969.

Borg, W.; Kelley, M.; Langer, P.; and Gall, M. *The Minicourse: A Microteaching Approach to Teacher Education.* Beverly Hills, Calif.: Macmillan Educational Services, 1970.

When microteaching appeared on the teacher education scene in 1963, it was viewed as a way to improve the often unstructured preservice teaching. It also would reduce the need for difficult-to-schedule teaching practice in schools. But most importantly, it was seen as a way to provide direct practice of important technical skills of teaching. In retrospect, it would seem that microteaching has more than met its original purposes and serves as an unusually promising instructional alternative in teacher education. It is well accepted by students. It provides a much needed form of direct experience with a model of reality in which controls and supervision can be exercised. Potentially it can familiarize preservice teachers with teaching skills associated with pupil academic achievement and satisfaction. Finally, the behaviors learned therein seem amenable to transfer and use in natural classrooms.

Simulations

At about the same time that researchers at Stanford University were developing microteaching, one person in Oregon, and a few years later several persons in New York, Tennessee, and Ohio were developing an instructional alternative to the preparation of teachers called simulation. The purpose of simulations is to prepare preservice students for some of the more challenging realities of classroom life. Prior to the advent of simulation, preservice students were sometimes told "war stories" by their education professors but not permitted to engage in "mock combat." Thus when faced with the reality of student teaching, preservice students hardly knew what to expect and had only scant notion of how they would, or should, respond.

Cruickshank (1971*a* , 1971*b*) discusses several simulations used in teacher education. The first one, called "Classroom Simulation," was developed by Kersh (1962) under a National Defense Education Grant at the Teaching Research Laboratory of the Oregon State System of Higher Education. This simulation uses a specially constructed mock classroom facility in which an elementary education student teacher, following orientation to a hypothetical school and sixth-grade classroom, is shown up to 60 filmed classroom problems. After each problem is presented, the student teacher is asked to act out or talk out a response. An experimenter sitting nearby considers the student teacher's response and decides how the class or a student therein probably would react. The experimenter then projects a film segment of the class or student reaction for the student teacher to see. The intention of the simulation is to shape a student teacher's behavior in ways that juries of master teachers feel are optimal.

Two other simulations of classrooms were developed in the late 1960s. Unlike Kersh's simulation, both of these were produced for commercial distribution. The *Teaching Problems Laboratory* (TPL) was developed under a U.S. Office of Education Cooperative Research Grant at the State University of New York College at Brockport (Cruickshank, Broadbent, and Bubb 1967). *Inner-City Simulation Laboratory* (ICSL) was developed a few years later at the University of Tennessee and Ohio State University (Cruickshank 1969).

The *TPL* is used with an entire class of preservice students. Following orientation to a hypothetical suburban elementary school, each student takes on the role of fifth-grade teacher Pat Taylor. They then are presented with up to 31 critical teaching problems that were gleaned from a survey of first-year teachers. The problems are presented through short films, written incidents, and role plays. After each problem is presented, each Pat Taylor is asked independently to 1) identify and define the problem; 2) identify factors that seem to be contributing to the problem; 3) locate pertinent related information; 4) project alternative courses of action that might resolve the problem; 5) select the most desirable course of action, the one with the fewest negative side effects; and 6) communicate or implement a decision. Following 15 to 20 minutes of independent problem solving utilizing the materials provided, the several Pat Taylors interact with each other in groups of four to six, projecting their individual perspectives and solutions for inspection and reflection. Finally, each problem and the issues involved are explored by the whole class.

The group feedback process of *TPL* encourages students to consider a greater variety of response strategies to the classroom problems they have identified, and provides them with opportunities to learn about and practice a wide variety of professional activities associated with problems of first-year teachers, such as test construction, parent conferencing, teaching difficult lessons, and developing a reading program.

The *Inner-City Simulation Laboratory* (ICSL) is similar to *TPL*, except that its locale is an inner-city school and classroom modeled after a school in Chicago and the problems presented were gleaned from a study of inner-city teachers. Several other simulations for use in teacher education are described in Cruickshank (1971a, 1971b), and a more up-to-date listing is in Cruickshank and Telfer (1979).

Identification of teacher problems and problem solving are central to the simulation process used in teacher education. The problems recreated in both *TPL* and *ICSL* were identified from field surveys. With *TPL*, this was done by a review of the literature on problems of beginning teachers. From that review a 117-item questionnaire was devised representing seven problem areas: discipline, evaluation, methods, parent relations, personal planning, routines, and materials. The instrument was used with 163 recent graduates of the State University of New York College at Brockport. Analysis of the responses indicated that 35 of the original 117 items could be considered significant and worthy of attention in the preservice program.

With *ICSL*, problem identification was done by practicing teachers in inner-city elementary schools, who kept daily, diary-like accounts of the "biggest problem" that caused them the greatest concern. Analysis of these diary-like accounts revealed that they could be reduced to 184 problems. The 184 problems served as a basis for developing an instrument. In the second phase of the study, the frequency and severity of each item on the instrument was responded to by the 287 teachers in the phase one schools. Analysis of their responses indicated that 96 of the problems could be considered significant on either the frequency or severity scales. Eighty were significant on both scales, and 45 were reported by more than one-third of the respondents as either frequent, severe, or both. These 45 fell within nine problem areas: disruptive student behavior, student home conditions, parent-school relationships, working with exceptional children, providing for individual differences, child-to-child relationships, building skills in independent work, school conditions, and child self-concepts.

These survey studies, Cruickshank and Broadbent (1965); Cruickshank and Leonard (1967); and Cruickshank, Kennedy, Leonard, and Thurman (1968), provided substantial verification of what are the perceived problems of teachers. Thus they can serve as a basis for designing authentic simulations.

More recent studies, Cruickshank, Kennedy, and Myers (1974) and Myers, et al. (1975), further confirm the problems of teaching practice. Theory related to five persistent areas of teacher concern (affiliation, control, parent relationships, student success, and time) represented in the simulations is discussed in *Teaching Is Tough* (Cruickshank, Applegate, Holton, Mager, Myers, Novak, and Tracey 1980).

Reaction to Simulation. Like microteaching, simulation has been generally well accepted by the teacher education community. Johnson (1968), prior to publication of *ICSL*, found that simulations were used to some extent in 72% of the 847 student teaching programs responding to his questionnaire. (The figure for microteaching was 44%.) Sherwin (1974) reported that simulations were used to some extent in 92% of the 719 AACTE institutions responding to her questionnaire. (The figure for microteaching was 94%.) Data provided by Joyce et al. (1977) indicate that simulations were used to some extent by 40%

of the 147 teacher education units reporting. (The figure for microteaching was 38%.)

There are several reasons for the good reception of simulations in teacher education programs. Because simulations frequently use realistic media, they provide preservice students with a form of firsthand experience in which to apply theory to practice in the safety of a model of reality. Further, since the simulation problems have been validated from practice, students and their instructors regard them as realistic models of what teaching is. Also, not to be overlooked is the fact that the use of simulations came on the heels of expanded federal support enabling teacher education institutions to develop or to purchase the requisite materials.

Research on Simulations. Unlike microteaching, little research has been conducted on simulations. It is more difficult to assess outcomes in simulations. Whereas proficiency in the technical skills of microteaching are observable and measurable, proficiency in problem solving promoted by simulations is more difficult to observe and measure.

Using the "Classroom Simulator," Kersh conducted an experiment to determine the impact of realism in the audiovisual presentation of classroom problems. The factors he investigated were size of image (small versus large) and motion (moving versus still). Results of the study provided mild support for small, still (slide) projection when the outcome measure was number of practice trials required to shape desired subject behavior (Kersh 1963).

Using a reproduction of Kersh's "Classroom Simulator," Vlcek (1965) studied 1) the effect of the simulator on preservice students in identifying and solving classroom problems prior to student teaching; 2) the transfer value of the experience, 3) the effect of the simulator on trainee self-confidence and ability to teach, and 4) trainee attitudes toward the simulation experience. Results of the study support the following conclusions:

1. Awareness of classroom problems is not enhanced through use of the "Classroom Simulator" as used in the study;
2. Effective responses to classroom problems can be shaped through engagement in the "Classroom Simulator";
3. Principles that are useful in solving classroom problems can be developed in the "Classroom Simulator";
4. Experience with a greater number of simulated classroom problems transfers to the student teaching experience;
5. Application of principles in solving classroom problems transfers to the student teaching experience; and
6. Preservice students' confidence in ability to teach is increased.

Further study of the "Classroom Simulator" revealed that realism in simulation and prompting is not as important in enhancing transfer of learning from the simulator to natural settings as are instructor differences and length of training (Twelker 1966).

Using the simulation prototype for the *Teaching Problems Laboratory*, Cruickshank and Broadbent (1968) conducted a study to judge its effectiveness in presenting teaching problems and to judge whether exposure to teaching problems had an observable effect on trainees' subsequent behavior during student teaching. Results of the study indicate that simulation is effective in presenting classroom problems. Further, exposure to simulated problems results in trainees having fewer problems during student teaching. Results do not support the hypotheses that trainees' general student teaching performance improves, that they are more confident, that they are able to assume full-time classroom responsibility sooner, or that they develop more positive feelings about teaching.

Gaffga (1967), using one of the field trials conducted by Cruickshank and Broadbent, found that trainee behavior in the simulation is similar to behavior during student teaching and is a better predictor of student teaching performance than ratings by education professors who have had the trainees in classes. Results of research on other teacher education simulations are found in Cruickshank (1971*b*).

Advantages and Disadvantages. Specific advantages of simulations as an instructional alternative, when used in conjunction with student teaching or as a campus-based laboratory experience, are:

1. They permit student teachers to work toward the resolution of problems of beginning teachers that normally do not surface in structured student teaching classrooms with a cooperating teacher present.
2. They afford student teachers opportunities to try to resolve classroom problems themselves rather than watching how someone else does so.
3. They permit the identification of potential student teacher needs so that they might be addressed and remedied as part of student teaching.
4. They offer opportunities for student teachers to work together on resolving problems they will commonly encounter and to share and reflect on current classroom concerns.

When used in conjunction with courses in humanistic and behavioral studies and in teaching and learning theory, simulations offer the following advantages:

1. They permit study of an educational setting — neighborhood, school, and classroom — in the manner of a behavioral scientist, that is, one who observes, describes, and attempts to understand.
2. They encourage preservice students to apply what they have learned in education courses to life in classrooms.
3. They can substitute for unstructured field experiences in schools and classrooms where the purposes and outcomes are unclear.
4. They permit identification of preservice students who by temperament

or preparation may not be well suited for student teaching or teaching at all.

Among the disadvantages of simulations cited are:

1. They are not real situations; therefore participants may not take their roles too seriously.
2. They may not elicit the same behavior from participants that they would demonstrate in a natural classroom.
3. They require college instructors who can guide preservice students in identifying and applying theoretical knowledge to life in classrooms.
4. They usually contain many components and therefore require special handling and care.

Materials to Support Simulation. Following is a selected list of resources useful to those wishing to implement simulations in teacher education.

Buffie, E., and Trojcak, D. *Simulation: A Program of Instruction Focusing upon the Human Relations Dimension of Teaching and the Decision-Making Process.* Bloomington: Center for Innovation in Teacher Education, School of Education, Indiana University, 1970.

Cantrell, W., and Edwards, A. *A Computer-Based Instructional Simulation for Teacher Training and Evaluation in Special Education.* University Park: College of Education, Pennsylvania State University, 1974.

Champaigne, D., and Goldman, R. "Simulation Activities for Training Parents and Teachers as Educational Partners." Paper presented at the annual meeting of the American Educational Research Association in New York, 1971.

Cruickshank, D. *Inner-City Simulation Laboratory.* Chicago: Science Research Associates, 1969.

Cruickshank, D.; Broadbent, F.; and Bubb, R. *Teaching Problems Laboratory.* Chicago: Science Research Associates, 1967.

Day, H., and Parnes, R. "A Computer-Based Simulation as an Alternative Teacher Training Strategy." Paper presented at the annual meeting of the American Educational Research Association in Washington, D.C., 1975.

Flake, J. *Interactive Computer Simulation — A New Component in Teacher Education.* Charleston: Eastern Illinois University, 1973.

Kersh, B. "The Classroom Simulator." *Journal of Teacher Education* 13 (1962): 109-110.

Lehman, D. "Simulation in Science — A Preliminary Report on the Use and Evaluation of Role Playing in the Preparation of Secondary School Student Teachers of Science." Paper presented at the annual meeting of the American Association for the Advancement of Science in Washington, D.C., 1966.

Meehan, D. "An Evaluation of Simulations as an Approach to Assisting Elementary Teachers to Identify Children with Learning Disabilities and to

Utilize Ancillary Personnel in Initiating Remediation Programs Within Their Classrooms." Doctoral dissertation, Syracuse University, 1971.

Morsink, C. "LRNG to Read: A Simulation for Teacher Training." *Journal of Learning Disabilities* 6, no. 7 (1973): 14-20.

Swan, H., and Johnson, J. *Simulation Exercises*. DeKalb, Ill.: Creative Educational Materials, 1968.

Swigger, K. "Computer-Based Simulations and Tutorials for Analyses and Improvement of Teachers' Questioning Skills." Doctoral dissertation, University of Iowa, 1977.

Teaching Research. *Low-Cost Instructional Simulation Materials for Teacher Education: Phase I and Phase II*. Monmouth: Oregon State System of Higher Education, 1968.

University of Massachusetts. *Instructional Planning Simulation*. Amherst, Mass.: School of Education, 1970.

University of Massachusetts. *School Communications Game*. Amherst, Mass.: School of Education, 1970.

Venditti, F. *Handbook for Teaching in Valleybrook Elementary School: A Simulation Game Focusing upon Problems of Racially Desegregated Schools*. Knoxville: Equal Opportunities Planning Center, University of Tennessee, n.d.

Wolfe, R. *Simulation: A Performance-Based Program for Supervising Teachers*. Washington, D.C.: ERIC Document Reproduction Service, 1973. (No. ED 086 655)

In summary, simulations provide opportunities for preservice teachers to learn about teaching by engaging in models of classrooms. They provide a safe setting and substantially greater control and direction over field experiences than can be provided in natural classrooms. Potentially, they can acquaint preservice teachers with almost any aspect of school or classroom reality. The simulations used most frequently permit preservice teachers to experience classroom problems and to practice problem solving and theory application. Both preservice teachers and selected teacher educators have found simulations to be effective instructional alternatives.

Protocol Materials

At the close of the 1960s a book by Smith et al. (1969) prompted the then U.S. Office of Education to provide substantial financial support during the first part of the next decade to develop protocol materials as an instructional alternative in preservice teacher education.

The rationale underlying the use of protocol materials was presented by Smith and his associates as follows:

> Teachers fail because they have not been trained calmly to analyze new situations against a firm background of relevant theory. Typically they

base their interpretations of behavior on intuition and common sense. . . . If the teacher is incapable of understanding classroom situations, the actions he takes will often increase his difficulties. (pp. 28-29)

For example, a teacher may be faced with pupil cheating. The teacher may become angry, aggressive, and resort to punishment. Such teacher responses may stop the behavior for the moment, but they do nothing to address the factors that caused the cheating. The teacher responds to the symptoms but does nothing to keep the behavior from reoccurring. The purpose of protocol materials is to get preservice teachers to analyze significant situations calmly, basing their analysis on something beyond intuition and common sense.

A protocol is an original record of an event (pupil cheating). At first Smith's intent was for each protocol to be an original record of an event that occurred naturally in a school or classroom. He later backed away from requiring original records and accepted contrived or simulated events because they were easier to prepare. As the event occurs, it is recorded, filmed, or transcribed in writing in the manner of an eye-witness news account, without editorializing.

Following the recording of the event, it is reviewed by the instructor to determine what related knowledge is necessary to illuminate the event for the preservice teacher. For example, if the event were pupil cheating, the instructor would look to the fields of psychology and sociology for information and concepts that offer empirical support for understanding cheating behavior in a variety of settings including classrooms. After the protocol is presented to preservice teachers, they are then guided in analyzing the event and in applying the appropriate related theory.

Since the events portrayed in the protocol are central, a discussion of how they are selected follows. Events depicted in protocols are intended to be *events of educational significance*, those that would be critical for preservice teachers to experience vicariously and to understand prior to experiencing them in natural classrooms. Smith et al. (1969) suggest that events of educational significance can come from classroom instructional situations such as management and control, as well as situations that arise while planning school programs, working with peers and administrators, working with parents and other members of the community, and working in professional organizations.

As the protocols movement in teacher education gained momentum, another framework was suggested for selecting events to be depicted in protocols. In contrast to Smith's selection of events of educational significance, this framework defined protocols as *illustrations of concepts* of educational significance (Cruickshank 1974). Furthermore, the new framework called for protocols to be developed for both the pedagogical domain and for the basic fields of knowledge. Accordingly,

protocol materials to be developed in the pedagogical domain should be concerned with the art of teaching and of learning, with the behavior of teachers, learners and teachers, and learners in interaction. In contrast protocol materials in the domain of the basic fields of knowledge should be concerned with the content of what is taught — or more specifically, with the knowledge about the knowledge that is taught. (Cruickshank 1974, p. 304)

Under this framework, protocol developers no longer had to pay attention to critical *events* occurring in the real world of teaching; now they could simply select and illustrate *concepts* typically mentioned in education texts. Such textbook concepts may be germane to teachers; but as teachers frequently have told us, often they are not. Consequently, the approximately 140 separate protocols developed under federal programs may be less related to critical aspects of life in classrooms than to typical textbook theory, which may or may not be on target.

Reaction to Protocol Materials. Protocols probably are less well known and less used than other instructional alternatives described here. Certainly protocols have value. If used as originally intended, they provide experience (albeit secondhand) with critical aspects of reality, they encourage higher-order thinking, and they provide a way of translating theory into practice. Indeed, they provide a quasi-clinical setting where preservice teachers engage in at least diagnosis if not prescription. An additionally attractive attribute of protocols is that they frequently make use of media.

We can only speculate why the use of protocols has not caught on in teacher education circles. Maybe because they are not readily available, teacher educators do not know about them. Maybe they are not seen as illustrating truly realistic events or basic concepts in teaching. Maybe teacher educators are not sure where or how to use them. Maybe teacher educators feel they have insufficient time to use them or have found them less useful than they expected.

Research on Protocol Materials. Since protocol materials did not arrive on the teacher education scene until the 1970s, most of the effort has been given to their development rather than to their evaluation. According to Copeland (1982, p. 1012), evaluators of protocol materials largely have been interested in determining whether, after using a protocol to introduce an educational concept, teacher education students can recognize that concept in operation when shown a film of a classroom in action (Berliner et al. 1973; Borg 1973; Gliessman and Pugh 1976; Kleucker 1974; Pugh and Gliessman 1976). The results of such evaluations, notes Copeland, "are certainly encouraging" in that they seem to confirm that concepts can be learned using protocols. However, he reminds us that what we eventually need to determine is whether preservice students who have learned the concepts are able to use them to guide their practice when they move into natural classrooms.

Advantages and Disadvantages. The advantages of protocol materials include the following:

1. They permit preservice teachers to experience vicariously events or concepts of educational significance;
2. They provide controlled observation and analysis of the events experienced;
3. They encourage acquisition of knowledge and interpretation of theory related to the event or concept;
4. They discourage over-dependency on personal experience when reacting to life in classrooms.

The major disadvantages of protocol materials are:

1. There is confusion about what protocols are or should be. Smith originally intended them to be records of educationally significant events to be studied and illuminated by the use of related theory. As later developed, they became records of the theory or concepts that presumably would illuminate classroom life.
2. They are time-consuming to use and relatively expensive to develop.
3. They require college instructors who are interested in and see value in studying life in classrooms that can be illuminated with related theory.
4. There is no consensus on what are the events of educational significance for which teachers should be prepared. Thus we do not have a firm foundation on which to develop protocols as envisioned originally by Smith in *Teachers for the Real World*.

Materials to Support Protocols. According to Cooper (1975), approximately 140 protocol products had been developed by 1975. Topics or concepts covered include: classroom management, self-concept, teacher language, classroom interaction, group process, pupil outcomes, instructional concepts, learning set, role concepts, children's language, creative responses to literature, developmental reading, and black dialect (Protocol Materials Catalog 1975). Protocol materials are distributed by the National Resource and Dissemination Center of the University of South Florida.

In summary, protocol materials could be characterized as a notion gone astray. As originally conceived, they could have brought a much needed change in teacher education that would provide a way for preservice students to use theory to illuminate classroom life; but what evolved was a much more didactic teaching device employing media to illustrate a concept. Nevertheless, the concept of protocol materials remains a potentially powerful one that could add an important dimension to instruction in preservice education.

Reflective Teaching

Reflective Teaching (RT) was conceptualized at Ohio State University and received support, beginning in 1978, from the Exxon Education Foundation and later from the George C. Gund Foundation and from Phi Delta Kappa. RT was born out of a desire to make available a form of on-campus, laboratory-clinical experience that combined many features of other instructional alternatives but would offer a different outcome. Microteaching gives practice in the technical skills of teaching. Simulations provide opportunity to resolve significant problems associated with teaching practice. Peer teaching provides experience in role playing teaching and learning. However, none of these instructional methods engage preservice students in the complete act of teaching, one in which they receive feedback about learner achievement and learner satisfaction and which would cause them to reflect thoughtfully on the teaching and learning that occurred. In essence, RT is an effort to increase teacher wisdom by engaging preservice students in controlled, on-campus teaching where their behavior is observable and measurable and where their teaching can be examined and thought about in ways that will enhance subsequent performance.

Ordinarily RT procedes as follows. A class of preservice students is divided into groups of four to six members each. One member of each group is appointed "designated teacher." The several designated teachers then are given a common Reflective Teaching Lesson (RTL) to prepare to teach in any way they wish to their group at an upcoming class meeting. The college instructor next makes certain that the designated teachers are clear about their goals, which are to bring about learner achievement and satisfaction and to guide their group in discussion of a set of questions about the teaching-learning event.

On the day of their teaching, designated teachers are assigned teaching stations and given a few minutes to set up. On signal from the instructor, all designated teachers begin to teach, employing any instructional approach they wish. After 15 minutes teaching is stopped and learners are given a "test" and complete a learner satisfaction form. Using their data on learner achievement and satisfaction, the designated teachers then guide their groups through the first of two reflective sessions, where the intent is to get participants to think about teaching and learning. After 15 minutes of small-group reflection, the college instructor assembles the participants into a large group for further exploration of the teaching-learning process.

Since the RTLs are central to the Reflective Teaching method, they require a bit more elaboration. Thirty-six RTLs have been developed and published (Cruickshank, Holton, Fay, Williams, Kennedy, Myers, and Hough 1981). Each meets five criteria:

1. It must be interesting to teach and to learn.
2. The content must be different from the usual academic curriculum.
3. The lesson must be brief enough to be successfully taught in 15 minutes or less.
4. The outcomes must be directly observable and measurable.
5. The lesson must be self-contained and must include all materials necessary for instruction.

A sampling of RTL titles includes: "The Chisanbop Task," a Korean method of computation that uses fingers and hands as calculators; "The Origami Task," Japanese paper folding; and "The Good Teacher Task," attributes of effective teachers.

RTLs are both ends in themselves and means to an end. As ends in themselves, RTLs engage participants in the complete act of teaching and give them feedback about learner achievement and learner satisfaction. RTLs are means to an end in that they provide a teaching-learning experience that can be examined or reflected upon. Reflection could not occur without an RTL.

The substance of the reflective sessions is the cognitive and affective experience of the designated teachers and their learners. Participants *must* reflect about the experience in order to develop good habits of thought about teaching. Specifically, the aim is to ask questions that cause participants to think about teaching and learning so that they will become wiser teachers. Among the outcomes of the reflective sessions are that the prospective teachers become more aware of the determinants of their teaching behavior, more open-minded and less opinionated, more likely to recognize and respond to the diversity of learners, more aware of the complexity of the teaching environment, more able to anticipate what an educational experience might be like for learners, more likely to teach in a way that maximizes benefits for learners, and more interested in their own professional growth.

The key to the reflective session is the questions asked. By asking the "right" questions following an RTL, we can maximize thoughtfulness and increase wisdom. Although the questions originally used in RT were developed without benefit of research, they later were substantiated (Cruickshank, Kennedy, Williams, Holton, and Fay 1981).

Reactions to Reflective Teaching. Acceptance of RT as an on-campus laboratory experience is high. For preservice students RT satisfies their desire to learn to teach by teaching. They prefer direct, firsthand experiences where they are the major role takers. Additionally, preservice teachers enjoy the professional and social interaction the reflective sessions provide. Following are some student comments given to a college instructor following use of RT.

> *RT provided me with an opportunity to formulate and try out my ideas about teaching.*
>
> *I found out that a great amount of preparation is necessary to be a good teacher.*
>
> *RT helped me to appreciate teaching and learning by experiencing both.*
>
> *I became more aware of myself as a teacher.*
>
> *I came to realize that students do not learn at the same pace and in the same way.*

I became aware that there are several ways to successfully teach the same lesson.

RT made me feel more confident in my ability to teach.

I became more aware of frustrations learners feel.

I learned I must be more clear.

RT provided me with an opportunity to see if I could really get students to learn.

I learned that knowing your subject is important.

I experienced what it was like to be a teacher.

I learned some of my strengths and weaknesses.

I learned that a teacher can not assume that because she is teaching, learners are learning.

I learned about how I felt about teaching as a career.

RT was probably the most beneficial learning experience that I was provided during this course.

RTLs are a lot of fun and a great experience for me.

Teacher educators also regard Reflective Teaching as having significant benefits. It provides an on-campus laboratory for the practice and examination of teaching. It permits several students to teach concurrently toward common objectives in the same classroom, thus increasing opportunity to share the experience. It provides opportunity to teach in cognitive, psychomotor, and affective domains. It can be used in a variety of courses and contexts. And it does not require expensive equipment or special personnel. Selected teacher educator comments about RT follow:

Reflective Teaching is an ingenious and useful addition to . . . teaching experiences. It has great face validity, it is inexpensive, it presents a controlled situation that permits useful opportunities for . . . analysis. (Robert Egbert, University of Nebraska)

Reflective Teaching is an approach based squarely on a professional model. (Donald Medley, University of Virginia)

Reflective Teaching has been well received by both faculty and students. We have written 18 additional Reflective Teaching Lessons. (William M. Nelson and others, Kearney State College, Nebraska)

The more I use it with our students, the more impressed I become. (Jerry Peters, Purdue University)

Its real value is the way its structure invites generalization from what happens [during Reflective Teaching] to what happens in school classrooms. (Thomas R. Rosebrough, Trevecca Nazarene College)

I'm especially impressed with the effect on students' understanding of the variety of teaching strategies that can be used to promote learning. (Claudia Cornett, Wittenberg University)

The students seem to benefit from the experience. They seem able to look at themselves as potential teachers and begin a self-evaluation that is non-threatening. (James Gay, University of Dayton)

I value reflectivity as an indispensable component of good teaching. . . . Reflective Teaching seems to have a particular potential for institutions [having] minimal opportunity for field experiences. (Robert Mulder, Wittenberg University)

Teacher education organizations have promoted RT's dissemination and use. Among others, the AACTE report *Educating a Profession: Profile of a Beginning Teacher* (Scannell et al. 1983) calls for use of RT. The Association of Teacher Educators sponsored a national clinic on RT and held a session on RT at its annual meeting in 1982 in Florida. Phi Delta Kappa has published the RT materials (Cruickshank, Holton, Fay, Williams, Kennedy, Myers, and Hough 1981) and from 1982 to 1984 sponsored almost 30 chapter workshops in order to acquaint members with its potential.

Two foundations have supported the development of RT materials. The Exxon Education Foundation made four grants to develop and field test the materials, to produce a 30-minute film *Reflective Teaching*, to produce a brochure announcing the film and support workshops on RT for teacher educators in Australia, and to write a book on RT. The George C. Gund Foundation made a grant to support four RT workshops to train Ohio teacher educators in its use.

Research on Reflective Teaching. Little research on RT has been done. The results of a limited evaluation of RT outcomes are presented in Cruickshank, Kennedy, Holton, Williams, and Nott (1980) and Cruickshank, Kennedy, Williams, Holton, and Fay (1981). In that study the principal claim, that RT promotes preservice students' ability to think and hence to express themselves in a complex manner when discussing the act of teaching and the process of learning, is partially supported. In addition, modest support is shown for positive change in student affect toward future student teaching. Specifically, students who had at least one opportunity to teach during RT reported that they were relatively less anxious than students not having RT experience. The research potential of RT is reported in Cruickshank (1984).

Materials Supporting Reflective Teaching. Below is a list of resources useful for persons who wish to learn more about using RT.

"Alternative Inservices: Thinking About Teaching." *Communication Quarterly* (Winter 1981): 3.

Applegate, J. "Reflective Teaching and Staff Development: A Partnership for Professional Growth." *The Developer* (April 1982): 1-8.

Cruickshank, D.R. "Benefits and Uses of Reflective Teaching." *Phi Delta Kappan* (in press).

Cruickshank, D. R. *The George C. Gund Foundation Sponsored Dissemination of Reflective Teaching to Ohio Teacher Educators: Final Report.* Columbus: Ohio State University, 1982.

Cruickshank, D. R. "Reflective Teaching: A New Instructional Alternative for Use in Teacher Education and Research on Teaching." In *Action in Teacher Education: A Responsible Program for the Eighties.* Ohio Confederation of Teacher Education Organizations, 1981, pp. 16-23.

Cruickshank, D. R., and Applegate, J. "Reflective Teaching as a Strategy for Teacher Growth." *Educational Leadership* 38, no. 7 (April 1981): 553-554.

Cruickshank, D. R., and Clausen, C. *Reflective Teaching* (film). Columbus: Ohio State University, Department of Photography and Cinema, 1983.

Cruickshank, D. R., and Kennedy, J. "Evaluation of Reflective Teaching Outcomes." *Journal of Education Research* 75, no. 1 (September-October 1981): 20-32.

Cruickshank, D. R.; Holton, J.; Fay, D.; Williams, J.; Kennedy, J.; Myers, B.; and Hough, B. *Reflective Teaching.* Bloomington, Ind.: Phi Delta Kappa, 1981.

In summary Reflective Teaching permits participants to teach, to determine learner achievement and learner satisfaction, and to examine the experience in a way that develops good habits of thought and teacher wisdom. Its benefits as perceived by preservice teachers, their mentors, and professional organizations are positive. The little research done on RT has been promising in that it supports the goal of promoting good habits of thought about teaching.

Summary Recommendations

In Part III we have addressed several questions relating to teaching method and instructional alternatives. Four promising instructional alternatives for use in preservice education have been defined operationally. Following are some recommendations for improving preservice instruction.

We must ensure that teacher educators are thoroughly familiar with the concept of teaching method and that preservice teachers can acquire the requisite knowledge and skills for effective classroom teaching.

We must ensure that teacher educators are aware of available instructional alternatives and have the ability to use them appropriately in the teacher education curriculum.

We should promote the continued use of available instructional alternatives and encourage more research on them.

We should develop additional instructional alternatives for use in various facets of the preservice teacher education curriculum.

We should compile and classify instructional materials for use in teacher education and make them available in faculty libraries in teacher education institutions.

Instruction in teacher education can be improved. Teacher educators, by preparation and experience, are capable of bringing about this improvement. What is needed is something that would energize teacher educators to teach as well as they know how.

References for Part III

Allen, D.; Bush, R.; Ryan, K.; and Cooper, J. *Teaching Skills for Elementary and Secondary Teachers.* New York: General Learning Corporation, 1969.

Allen, D., and Ryan, K. *Microteaching.* Reading, Mass.: Addison-Wesley, 1969.

Berliner, D. "Impediments to the Study of Teacher Effectiveness." *Journal of Teacher Education* 27, no. 1 (1976): 5-14.

Berliner, D.; Golden, G.; Bierly, M.; Codori, C.; Hunter, L.; Loeding, D.; and Porteus, K. *Protocols on Group Process.* San Francisco: Far West Laboratory for Educational Research and Development, 1973.

Bierly, M.; Clark, C.; Cozine, W.; Gage, N.; Havers, N.; Loeding, D.; Peterson, P.; Wessitsch, A.; Wisson, D.; Winne, P.; and Zifferblatt, S. *Teacher Training Products: The State of the Field.* Stanford, Calif.: Stanford Center for Research on Teaching, 1974.

Borg, W. "Protocols: Competency-Based Teacher Education Modules." *Educational Technology* 13 (1973): 17-20.

Broudy, H. "Historic Exemplars of Teaching Method." In *Handbook of Research on Teaching,* edited by N. L. Gage. Chicago: Rand McNally, 1963.

Cooper, J. "A Survey of Protocol Materials Evaluation." *Journal of Teacher Education* 26, no. 1 (1975): 69-77.

Copeland, W. "Laboratory Experiences in Teacher Education." In *Encyclopedia of Educational Research,* edited by H. Mitzel. New York: The Free Press, 1982.

Copeland, W. "Processes Mediating the Relationship Between Cooperating Teacher Behavior and Student Teacher Classroom Performance." *Journal of Educational Psychology* 70, no. 1 (1978): 95-100.

Copeland, W. "Some Factors Related to Student Teacher Classroom Performance Following Microteaching Training." *American Educational Research Journal* 14, no. 2 (1977): 147-57.

Copeland, W. "The Relationship Between Microteaching and Student Teaching

Classroom Performance." *Journal of Educational Research* 68 (1975): 289-93.

Cruickshank, D.R. "The Research Potential of Reflective Teaching." *Mid-Western Educational Researcher* 5, no. 2 (1984): 1-6.

Cruickshank, D.R. "The Protocol Materials Movement: An Exemplar of Efforts to Wed Theory and Practice in Teacher Education." *Journal of Teacher Education* 25, no. 4 (1974): 300-11.

Cruickshank, D.R. *Simulation as an Instructional Alternative in Teacher Preparation.* Washington, D.C.: Association of Teacher Educators and ERIC Clearinghouse on Teacher Education, 1971. (SP004977) (a)

Cruickshank, D.R. "Teacher Education Looks at Simulation." In *Educational Aspects of Simulation*, edited by P. Tansey. London: McGraw-Hill, 1971. (b)

Cruickshank, D.R. *Inner-City Simulation Laboratory.* Chicago: Science Research Associates, 1969.

Cruickshank, D.R.; Applegate, J.; Holton, J.; Mager, J.; Myers, B.; Novak, C.; and Tracey, K. *Teaching Is Tough.* Englewood Cliffs, N.J.: Prentice-Hall, 1980.

Cruickshank, D.R., and Broadbent, F. *The Simulation and Analysis of Beginning Teachers.* Final Report, U.S. Department of Health, Education and Welfare Project No. 5-0798. Washington, D.C., 1968.

Cruickshank, D.R., and Broadbent, F. "The Identification and Analysis of Problems of First Year Teachers." In *Educational Research and Contemporary Social Problems.* Albany: State University of New York, 1965. (ERIC Document Reproduction Service No. ED 024 637)

Cruickshank, D.R.; Broadbent, F.; and Bubb, R. *The Teaching Problems Laboratory.* Chicago: Science Research Associates, 1967.

Cruickshank, D.R.; Clingen, M.; and Peters, J. "The State of the Art of Simulation in Teacher Education." *Simulations/Games for Learning* 9, no. 2 (1979): 72-82.

Cruickshank, D.R.; Holton, J.; Fay, D.; Williams, J.; Kennedy, J.; Myers, B.; and Hough, B. *Reflective Teaching.* Bloomington, Ind.: Phi Delta Kappa, 1981.

Cruickshank, D.R.; Kennedy, J.; Holton, J.; Williams, J.; and Nott, D. "A Summative Evaluation of the Outcomes of Reflective Teaching." In *Reflective Teaching: Project Final Report to the Exxon Education Foundation.* Columbus: Ohio State University College of Education, September 1980.

Cruickshank, D.R.; Kennedy, J.; Leonard, J.; and Thurman, R. *Perceived Problems of Teachers in Schools Serving Rural Disadvantaged Populations: A Comparison with Problems Reported by Inner-City Teachers.* Washington, D.C.: American Association of Colleges for Teacher Education, 1968. (ERIC Document Reproduction Service No. ED 127 986)

Cruickshank, D.R.; Kennedy, J.; and Myers, B. "Perceived Problems of Secondary School Teachers." *Journal of Educational Research* 68, no. 4 (1974): 154-59.

Cruickshank, D.R.; Kennedy, J.; Williams, J.; Holton, J.; and Fay, D. "Evaluation of Reflective Teaching Outcomes." *Journal of Educational Research* 75, no. 1 (1981): 26-32.

Cruickshank, D.R., and Leonard, J. *The Identification and Analysis of Perceived Problems of Teachers in Inner-City Schools.* Washington, D.C.: American Association of Colleges for Teacher Education, 1967. (ERIC Document Reproduction Service No. ED 026 335)

Cruickshank, D.R., and Telfer, R. "Classroom Games and Simulations." *Theory Into Practice* 19, no. 1 (1980): 75-80.

Cruickshank, D.R., and Telfer, R. *Simulations and Games: An ERIC Bibliography.* Bibliographies in Education Topics Number 11. Washington, D.C.: ERIC Clearinghouse on Teacher Education, 1979.

Dale, E. *Audiovisual Methods in Teaching.* New York: Dryden Press, 1969.

de Bono, E. *Lateral Thinking: Creativity Step-by-Step.* New York: Harper & Row, Colophon Books, 1973.

Dodl, N.; Elfner, E.; Becker, J.; Halstead, J.; Jung, H.; Nelson, P.; Purinton, S.; and Wegele, P. *Catalog of Teacher Competencies.* Tallahassee: Florida State University, 1972.

Erickson, F., and Wilson, J. *Sights and Sounds of Life in Schools: A Resource Guide to Film and Videotape for Research and Education.* East Lansing: Institute for Research on Teaching, Michigan State University College of Education, 1982.

Gaffga, R. "Simulation: A Model for Observing Student Teacher Behavior." Doctoral dissertation, University of Tennessee, 1967.

Gage, N. L. "A Factorially Designed Experiment on Teacher Structuring, Soliciting and Reacting." *Journal of Teacher Education* 27, no. 1 (1976): 35-39.

Gall, M. "Competency-Based Teacher Education Materials: How Available? How Usable? How Effective?" *Journal of Teacher Education* 30, no. 3 (1979): 58-61.

Gliessman, D., and Pugh, R. "Research on the Rationale, Design, and Effectiveness of Protocol Materials." *Journal of Teacher Education* 29, no. 6 (1978): 87-91.

Gliessman, D., and Pugh, R. "The Development and Evaluation of Protocol Films of Teacher Behavior." *AV Communications Review* 24 (1976):21-48.

Houston, R.; Baden, D.; Burke, J.; Dodl, N.; Hall, G.; Houston, E.; Olmsted, L.; Schroeder, E.; and Weber, W. *Resources for Performance-Based Education.* Albany, N.Y.: State Education Department, 1973.

Houston, R.; Nelson, K.; and Houston, E. *Resources for Performance-Based Education: Supplement A.* Albany, N.Y.: State Education Department, 1973.

Howsam, R.B.: Corrigan, D.; Denemark, J.; and Nash, R. *Educating a Profession.* Washington, D.C.: American Association of Colleges for Teacher Education, 1976.

Hudgins, B. *Problem Solving in the Classroom.* New York: Macmillan, 1966.

Johnson, J. *A National Survey of Student Teaching Programs.* USEO Report No. 6-8182. Washington, D.C.: U.S. Office of Education, 1968.

Joyce, B.; Yarger, S.; Howey, K.; Harbeck, K.; and Kluwin, T. *Preservice Teacher Education.* Palo Alto, Calif.: Center for Educational Research and Development, 1977.

Kersh, B. *Classroom Simulation: A New Dimension in Teacher Education.* Final Report, Title VII Project No. 886. Washington, D.C.: U.S. Department of Health, Education and Welfare, 1963.

Kersh, B. "The Classroom Simulator." *Journal of Teacher Education* 13 (1962): 109-10.

Kleucker, J. "Effects of Protocol and Training Materials." In *Acquiring Teaching Competencies: Reports and Studies (No. 6),* edited by L. D. Brown. Bloomington: Indiana University, National Center for the Development of Training Materials in Teacher Education, 1974.

Maier, N. *Problem Solving and Creativity.* Belmont, Calif.: Wadsworth Publishing Co., 1970.

McDonald, F. "Behavior Modification in Teacher Education." In *The Seventy-Second Yearbook of the National Society for the Study of Education: Part II,* edited by C. Thoreson. Chicago: University of Chicago Press, 1973.

McKnight, P. "Development of the Technical Skills of Teaching 1968-1978 and Beyond." Paper presented at the annual meeting of the American Educational Research Association, 1978. (ERIC Document Reproduction Service No. ED 171 699)

Meierhenry, W. *Mediated Teacher Education Resources.* Washington, D.C.: American Association of Colleges for Teacher Education, 1970.

Myers, B.; Cruickshank, D. R.; and Kennedy, J. *Problems of Teachers Graduated from the Ohio State University as Teacher Education Curriculum Indicators.* Columbus: Ohio State University College of Education, 1975.

National Association of State Directors of Teacher Education and Certification. *Standards for State Approval of Teacher Education.* 1981 ed. Salt Lake City: Utah State Office of Education Staff Development Section, 1981.

National Council for Accreditation of Teacher Education. *Standards for the Accreditation of Teacher Education.* Washington, D.C., 1982.

National Education Association. *Inservice Education Project Interim Report to NEA Leaders.* Washington, D.C., n.d.

Peterson, P.; Marx, R.; and Clark, C. "Teacher Planning, Teacher Behavior and Student Achievement." *American Educational Research Journal* 15, no. 3 (1978): 417-32.

Protocol Materials Catalogue: 1975 Edition. Tallahassee: Florida State Department of Education, 1975. (ERIC Document Reproduction Service No. ED 100 993)

Pugh, R., and Gliessman, D. *Measuring the Effects of a Protocol Film Series: Instrument Development and Use.* Bloomington: Indiana University Center for Development in Teacher Education, 1976. (ERIC Document Reproduction Service No. ED 123 254)

Scannell, D.; Corrigan, D.; Denemark, G.; Dieterle, L.; Egbert, R.; and Nielson, R. *Educating a Profession: Profile of a Beginning Teacher.* Washington, D.C.: American Association of Colleges for Teacher Education, 1983.

Schmuck, R.; Chesler, M.; and Lippitt, R. *Problem Solving to Improve Classroom Learning.* Chicago: Science Research Associates, 1966.

Sherwin, S. *Teacher Education: A Status Report.* Princeton, N.J.: Educational Testing Service, 1974.

Smith, B. O.; Cohen, S.; and Pearl, A. *Teachers for the Real World.* Washington, D.C.: American Association of Colleges for Teacher Education, 1969.

Snow, R. "A Second Generation of Microteaching Skills Research." Draft of a paper presented at the annual meeting of the American Psychological Association in Washington, D.C., August 1969.

Twelker, P. "Prompting as an Instructional Variable in Classroom Simulation." Paper presented at the meeting of the American Educational Research Association in Chicago, 1966.

Vlcek, C. "Assessing the Effect and Transfer Value of a Classroom Simulator Technique." Doctoral dissertation, Michigan State University, 1965.

Part IV
Summing Up

This part contains a summary of recommendations for improving curriculum and instruction in preservice teacher education. The recommendations are presented according to the organization of the sections of the book.

The Teacher Education Curriculum

General Education

1. All stakeholders in teacher education should become more aware of the meaning and purpose of general education.

2. Teacher education scholars should give attention to the general education of prospective teachers.

3. Institutions preparing teachers should require them to take courses that meet the meaning and purpose of general education.

4. Preservice teachers should demonstrate that they have a good general education prior to being certified to teach.

Professional Education

5. Teacher educators should reach consensus on what constitutes the specialized or professional knowledge of the teacher education curriculum and on how it should be logically organized.

6. Once the teacher education curriculum is agreed on and logically organized, a decision must be made about the length of the program. In making this decision, consideration must be given to the possibility of an extended program beyond the traditional four-year baccalaureate sequence.

7. Prospective teachers should be well prepared in the subject field they will teach and in related subjects, and they should know how to teach their

subject to K-12 pupils. Relatedly, faculty preparing teachers in their subject field should be thoroughly familiar with K-12 curriculum and instruction. Prospective teachers should demonstrate mastery of their subject field and related subjects prior to being certified to teach.

8. Within the professional curriculum, preservice students should be well prepared to use knowledge from the humanistic and behavioral studies in such a way that the knowledge illuminates events and life in schools and classrooms. Preservice students should demonstrate their ability to utilize knowledge from the foundation areas when confronted with situations in classrooms and schools.

9. Prospective teachers should be well prepared in knowledge about teaching and knowledge about learning. They should be examined on their mastery of teaching and learning both by paper-and-pencil tests and by demonstration in controlled laboratory settings. Faculty who primarily instruct preservice students should be committed to preservice teacher preparation rather than graduate education or to an academic discipline. Relatedly, these faculty should have a broad understanding of the whole teacher education curriculum.

10. Preservice teachers should have laboratory and clinical experiences both on and off campus. The on-campus experiences should include microteaching, exploration and resolution of classroom problems via simulations, thoughtful consideration or examination of controlled teaching episodes such as in Reflective Teaching, and use of protocol materials. Off-campus experience in natural classrooms should be concerned more with quality than quantity, and they should be more laboratory and clinically oriented as in the professions than as apprenticeships in the building trades. Relatedly, there should be more attention given to precisely what is to be learned in the practicum or student teaching.

Other Curriculum Recommendations

11. All preservice curriculum formulations should be identified and summarized as a way of establishing a history of teacher education curricula.

12. A permanent national teacher education curriculum council should be formed and maintained as a way of ensuring ongoing concern for the preservice curriculum.

13. The various stakeholders in teacher education must get together and behind an effort toward overall preservice curriculum improvement. Inquiry in teacher education must be encouraged, and results of such inquiry should be a basis for determination of the curriculum.

14. A manual of clinical knowledge about teaching should be prepared.

15. Teacher educators should work toward reducing personal and vested curriculum interests and toward increasing efforts to provide the best possible curriculum for preservice candidates.

Alternative Teacher Education Curricula

1. Teacher educators and others with vested interests in the preservice curriculum should become familiar with alternative teacher education curricula.

2. Student teaching should be a truly clinical experience.

3. Preservice teachers should be made aware that the act of teaching can be analyzed and studied with an eye toward improving practice.

4. What is taught in the preservice curriculum should have obvious and direct transfer to the realities of classroom life.

5. Preservice students should be assisted in becoming their most effective selves as teachers rather than urging them to try to teach like someone else.

6. The preservice curriculum should be presented in a sequence consonant with the developmental stages of preservice students.

7. Preservice students should learn about teaching, in part, by taking roles as in the theater.

8. Preservice students should be prepared to deal with the broad diversity found in normal classrooms.

9. The theoretical component of teacher education should focus on understanding the complexities of school and classroom life.

10. Provision should be made in the preservice curriculum for consideration of teaching as a career, the study of technical skills of teaching, classroom situations, human development and learning, diagnosis of learning difficulties, problem solving, school and classroom dynamics, pupil evaluation, educational technology, teaching methods, and instructional alternatives.

11. The preservice curriculum should be based on observable and measurable competencies needed by the beginning teacher, such as assessing pupil behavior, planning instruction, instructing, and evaluation of teaching.

12. The curriculum should address multicultural education as preservice students must know and teach it.

13. Preservice students should study those undergirding disciplines that provide much of the knowledge base of education.

14. Attention should be given to problem solving and its application to areas of concern perceived by teachers: affiliation, control, parent relationships, student success, and time management.

15. Opportunity should be provided for controlled teaching with subsequent examination of it in order to help teachers to develop good habits of thought and to become students of teaching.

16. Knowledge and practice of effective teaching behaviors such as with-it-ness, smoothness, momentum, group alerting, praise, provision of incentives, direct instruction, monitoring pupil behavior, clarity, enthusiasm, and variability should become part of the curriculum.

17. Preservice teachers should study and practice how to facilitate learning, manage the classroom, and make professional decisions.

18. All alternative curriculum notions should be identified and summa-

rized so that the relationship of current curricula to the alternatives can be further analyzed. Relatedly, the development of a taxonomy of teacher education curricula should be pursued so as to provide a curriculum classification system.

Instruction in Teacher Education

1. All instructional alternatives available for use in preservice teacher education should be identified and categorized according to their purposes and attributes.

2. Prospective and practicing teacher educators should become familiar with the purposes and attributes of various instructional alternatives. They should have experience in using the alternatives in order to make informed decisions regarding their value, potential use, and possible improvement.

3. Preservice education should be made more like the professional models used in other professions by introducing substantial use of controlled clinical and laboratory experiences prior to experiences in natural classrooms.

4. An effort should be made to catalogue and make available alternative instructional materials that would seem most useful for improving instruction in preservice education. Relatedly, teacher education organizations should develop and maintain a repository for such materials.

5. The production of instructional alternative materials should be encouraged and rewarded, with guidelines for instructional needs provided to developers and publishers.

6. Instruction in preservice teacher education should be conducted only by persons with knowledge of and experience with the appropriate instructional alternatives.

Author Index